Social Skills Programmes
An Integrated Approach from Early Years to Adolescence

Social Skills Programmes

An Integrated Approach from Early Years to Adolescence

Maureen Aarons & Tessa Gittens

Illustrations by Guy Redhead

Speechmark Publishing Ltd
Telford Road, Bicester, Oxon OX26 4LQ, UK

First published in 2003 by
Speechmark Publishing Ltd, Telford Road, Bicester, Oxon OX26 4LQ, UK
Tel: +44 (0) 1869 244 644   Fax: +44 (0) 1869 320 040
www.speechmark.net

© Maureen Aarons & Tessa Gittens, 2003
Reprinted 2004, 2006

All rights reserved. The whole of this work, including all text and illustrations, is protected by copyright. No part of it may be copied, altered, adapted or otherwise exploited in any way without express prior permission, unless it is in accordance with the provisions of the Copyright Designs and Patents Act 1988 or in order to photocopy or make duplicating masters of those pages so indicated, without alteration and including copyright notices, for the express purposes of instruction and examination. No parts of this work may otherwise be loaded, stored, manipulated, reproduced, or transmitted in any form or by any means, electronic or mechanical, including photocopying and recording, or by any information, storage and retrieval system without prior written permission from the publisher, on behalf of the copyright owner.

002-4771/Printed in the United Kingdom/1030

British Library Cataloguing in Publication Data
Aarons, Maureen
 Social skills programmes : an integrated approach from early years to adolescence
 1. Social skills in children – Study and teaching   2. Socialization – Study and teaching
 3. Children with mental disabilities   4. Children with social disabilities.   5. Teenagers with mental disabilities   6. Teenagers with social disabilities
 I. Title   II. Gittens, Tessa
 302.3'4'083

ISBN-10: 0 86388 310 9
ISBN-13: 978 0 86388 310 1

Contents

Acknowledgements	VII
Note on the Text	VII
Introduction	IX

PART I: 3 TO 5 YEAR-OLDS	1
Setting the Scene	2
Parents' Workshop	4
SESSION 1: *Settling Down*	5
SESSION 2: *What Happens Next?*	8
SESSION 3: *Talk About*	10
SESSION 4: *Good Looking*	12
SESSION 5: *In, On, Under*	14
SESSION 6: *Good Listening*	16
SESSION 7: *In front of, Behind, Next to*	18
SESSION 8: *Think About Position*	20
SESSION 9: *Likes & Dislikes*	22
SESSION 10: *Saying Goodbye*	24

PART II: 5 TO 7 YEAR-OLDS	27
Setting the Scene	28
Teachers' Workshop	31
SESSION 1: *Observation & Awareness of Others*	32
SESSION 2: *Good Looking*	41
SESSION 3: *Good Listening*	50
SESSION 4: *Turn-Taking*	59
SESSION 5: *Revision: Looking, Listening, Turn-Taking*	68
SESSION 6: *Talk About*	69
SESSION 7: *Being Friends*	70
SESSION 8: *More About Friends*	79
SESSION 9: *How am I Doing?*	89
SESSION 10: *Having a Party – Saying Goodbye*	98

PART III: 7 TO 11 YEAR-OLDS — 99

General Introduction	100
SESSION 1: *Meetings & Greetings*	102
SESSION 2: *Manners*	104
SESSION 3: *More About Manners*	105
SESSION 4: *Friends*	106
SESSION 5: *More About Friends*	108
SESSION 6: *Feelings*	109
SESSION 7: *More About Feelings*	110
SESSION 8: *Meaning*	111
SESSION 9: *More About Meaning*	113
SESSION 10: *Reflecting*	115
Follow-on Sessions	116

PART IV: 11 TO 16 YEAR-OLDS
Older Children & Adolescents — 119

General Introduction	120
SESSION 1: *Group Rules & Why Are We Here?*	123
SESSION 2: *How Do We Feel?*	125
SESSION 3: *Body Language*	126
SESSION 4: *Conversation Skills*	127
SESSION 5: *Issues & Problems*	128
SESSION 6: *What Words Mean*	129
SESSION 7: *More About What Words Mean*	132
SESSION 8: *Having & Giving*	133
SESSION 9: *Out and About, & Shopping*	134
SESSION 10: *Party Time*	135
Follow-on Sessions	136

PART V: Appendixes — 139

Appendix I Forms	140
Appendix II Resources	157

ACKNOWLEDGEMENTS

We are indebted to all the children who have participated in our Social Skills groups over the years.

NOTE ON THE TEXT

Although we use the term 'parents', we wish to make it clear that this includes single parents, carers or anyone who is acting *in loco parentis*.

Please note that, for consistency of style, the pronoun 'he' is sometimes used when referring to children of both sexes.

For many children, it is not an absence of ability in these areas of social competence, but *qualitative* deficits in comparison with their socially normal peers.

Introduction

Social communication and the teaching of social skills has become a focus of interest for teachers, psychologists and speech & language therapists over recent years. This would seem to be in response to the increasing numbers of children with identifiable problems in this area. Additionally, changes in educational practice in relation to children with special educational needs and a move towards their inclusion in mainstream schools has meant that greater collaboration and a blurring of professional working boundaries is taking place. It is our intention to facilitate this process in a field in which we have a particular interest. Readers may already be familiar with our earlier publication *Autism: A Social Skills Approach for Children and Adolescents* (1998), in which we introduced the rationale that children with a social impairment require training in the area of social skills. Autism is unquestionably the disorder that is inextricably linked to social development problems. However, a diagnosis is not always available, or necessarily considered appropriate, when mild social impairments coexist with other difficulties, such as dyslexia or dyspraxia. It is our belief that a social skills approach is relevant to the needs of a much wider group of children than those with a diagnosis of an autistic disorder *per se*.

Although we subscribe to the view that a diagnostic context is useful for many different reasons, in practical terms it is far more constructive to tackle the evident social difficulties than debate diagnostic criteria, as so few children fall neatly into prescribed groups. Diagnosis is essentially a medical model. In education, diagnostic boundaries are less important than educational needs. In the process of carrying out social skills programmes, some professionals may well reach conclusions about diagnosis that will enhance their understanding of individual children. However, the benefits and effectiveness of the programmes are not dependent on the recognition of particular disorders.

Historically, teachers and speech & language therapists come from different perspectives. Speech & language therapists, in a profession allied to medicine, refer to patients and, more recently, clients. They prescribe intervention as treatment for a percentage of individuals with specific requirements, with the assumption that this will be episodic rather than ongoing, and will end sooner or later in discharge from the service. Teachers however, are required to deliver a curriculum as an ongoing responsibility, differentiated as appropriate, and without exception. This does not include the notion of progress followed by discharge. We wish to encourage a 'consensus' between the two disciplines, and the area of social skills is an ideal meeting place that can be developed in both mainstream and special school settings. The blurring of the boundaries between the professions can lead to stimulating and innovative working practices, which will certainly benefit the children. In the UK in particular, for the speech & language therapist there is the opportunity to become involved in adapting aspects of the social skills programme to coalesce with elements of the national curriculum, particularly with reference to personal, social, emotional and health education (PSHE), and to move away from treatment blocks towards the teaching model. For the teacher, a move towards a 'therapeutic' mode, with greater focus and attention to detail than is generally practical in the classroom, can be a very worthwhile and enriching experience. For both teacher and therapist, there is the opportunity to collaborate and develop a resource which would not have been possible without the mutual sharing of their individual expertise.

It would be wrong to imply that joint working practices can be developed without careful planning. Things will not just happen, and it is important that both teacher and therapist have a very clear idea of their areas of responsibility. For example:

- How will the children be selected?

- How will they be assessed?

- Who will liaise with parents?

- Who will be responsible for clerical administration?

- Who will write reports?

- How many children will be catered for in each group?

- Will there be a mix of age ranges within a group?

- Will it be possible to bring together children from different schools?

- If children do not fit into the framework, how will they be dealt with?

- Will both professionals be involved simultaneously?

- Will classroom/speech and language therapy assistants be involved?

- How will the children's progress be evaluated?

These are but a few of the points that will need clarification in advance of running the groups. Even within an ethos of collaboration there has to be some differentiation of roles, and much will depend on the individuals involved – for example, in their particular areas of expertise and experience. However, we make the following suggestions as guidelines rather than as a prescribed formula.

THE SPEECH & LANGUAGE THERAPIST

It would seem appropriate for the speech & language therapist to carry out assessments of language and communication, as this is part of their professional remit.

The speech & language therapist is likely to be aware of children with social difficulties in other schools and through contacts within the local NHS Trust, and he or she should be the key person in selecting children to form a group.

It may be more appropriate for the speech & language therapist to obtain developmental and diagnostic information from parents, as disclosing such information to teachers may be an area of sensitivity.

Because speech & language therapists are often peripatetic, they can be flexible and undertake visits and duties on an *ad hoc* basis. They could therefore take responsibility for dealing with specific parental concerns out of school hours and away from school premises.

THE TEACHER

Teachers can be relied on to assess children's social behaviour in the classroom and playground, and to evaluate their suitability for working in a small group.

Teachers are generally better placed to deal with the organisation of the group, as they have access to their school administrator and office resources – not least the telephone, photocopier and e-mail.

The teacher is also better placed to timetable the group to fit in with arrangements within the school. It would seem likely that the teacher would be responsible for school staffing issues – for example, cover and the use of classroom or support assistants.

The teacher may also be in a better position to deal with general day-to-day queries and concerns from parents.

AREAS FOR INTEGRATED WORKING AND COLLABORATION

- Parent workshops

- Selection of children for the group

- Programme-planning linked to the curriculum

- Homework goals and aims

- Evaluation of the content of programmes

- Progress-monitoring.

THE ROLE OF PARENTS

The teaching of social skills must relate to all aspects of a child's daily life. Therefore parents, or those caring for the child, have a vital and proactive part to play. This means that they must be involved at all stages of the programme, and unless they can make this commitment, their child's progress will be hindered.

Before the start of the group
Parents will be invited to participate in a workshop where they will learn about the aims of the group sessions and consider their child's present social functioning, so that realistic and relevant goals can be set.

Between the weekly sessions
Parents will be required to carry out homework tasks with their child and, with the help of a simple checklist, to monitor progress.

After the final session
Parents will receive feedback, and will be asked to evaluate the overall effectiveness of the group in relation to their child's needs. In order to generalise any improvements made by the child, the onus is on parents to maintain the skills that have been achieved, and to continue to monitor progress. In order to evaluate any changes or developments, parents will be required to complete a further questionnaire six months later. This will not only provide information about the effectiveness of this form of intervention, but will help determine whether a further social skills group might be helpful. As children mature there will inevitably be new demands and new difficulties: a child who benefited from an early years (at age 3 to 5 years) group may need further input between the ages of 7 and 11, and so on. Parental involvement will lessen as children become more independent as they reach their adolescence.

EVALUATING PROGRESS

Current practice for both teachers and speech & language therapists includes setting targets and assessing progress. Indeed, these procedures have assumed such importance in recent years that some professionals have begun to question whether this is at the expense of spontaneity and real vocation. Nevertheless, in terms of limited resources and value for money, there has to be some evaluation of intervention. As we have already mentioned, parents make a contribution to this process, which is of equal importance to that of the professionals. In order to make any sort of valid judgement about a child's progress, a baseline must be established. This should be a combination of results of standardised assessments where available or appropriate, and information about the child's social functioning in school or nursery, in conjunction with the views of the parents. Relevant forms for this purpose are included in Appendix 1 (Form 2).

Generally, brief descriptive comments are far more meaningful and useful than a scoring system, which simply ascribes a number to an aspect of a child's social functioning on a particular day, at a particular time. Changes or developments should be recorded after the child has completed the group programme: this will be a summary of routine weekly monitoring of the group (Form 5a). After a period of six months, the evaluation process should be repeated to ascertain whether there is evidence of progress, and whether that progress has been maintained and generalised (Form 5b).

WHICH CHILDREN ARE LIKELY TO BENEFIT FROM A SOCIAL SKILLS GROUP?

Criteria for suitability

A pre-school child is unlikely to benefit from a social skills group if he can only attend with close one-to-one supervision. There must be an ability to focus on activities not of his own choosing. Language comprehension should be at no less than a three-word level on, for example, a Derbyshire assessment. Pre-school children who satisfy these criteria will be more likely to have developed a level of cognitive understanding, which is necessary if they are to benefit from this kind of input.

Children of school age with social communication difficulties may have received speech and language therapy because of earlier delay in language acquisition. Many of these children subsequently progress well and achieve age-appropriate or near age-appropriate scores on standardised assessments of language. However, despite this progress, they fail to use language communicatively. Some children may appear very verbal when talking about their own interests, yet they too fail in this area of communication.

It will also become increasingly evident that their difficulties are not linked to language use alone, but in addition affect relationships and imagination. Many of these children have difficulties interacting with their peers and may be bullied, or claim to have no friends. Quite often the reason for this is that they have a capacity for annoying others, but with little awareness of the impact this has. Such things as reminding their peers of school rules; reporting on the misdemeanours of others, as well as inappropriate touching or intrusion into other children's space are the sorts of behaviours that are unlikely to endear them to their peers. Sadly, although they want to make friends, they have little idea how to go about acquiring them.

For many children it is not an absence of ability in these areas of social competence, but *qualitative* deficits in comparison with their socially normal peers. The essence of the children's problems is difficulty in extracting what is meaningful in the world about them, and in understanding the feelings and intentions of others. Some of these children may have a diagnosis of an autistic spectrum disorder, though the absence of a diagnosis does not mean that autism can be excluded.

Since language is the medium for working on social skills with these children, normal or near normal cognitive and language skills are necessary for the child to benefit from this kind of intervention. If, despite fulfilling all the criteria, a child's behaviour is consistently challenging or disruptive to the extent that it affects the successful functioning of the group, it is better to exclude such a child. Inclusion may be more successful at a later date.

It will be obvious to anyone reading the entire range of session plans from early years to adolescence that we have provided considerably more guidance for the older children. The reason for this is that social communication and social interaction become increasingly more demanding and complex, which in turn requires more detailed clarification and explanation.

USING THE PROGRAMMES

All the programmes can be used flexibly – for example, the 3 to 5 years' programme can be used for older children with a cognitive disability as long as the criteria relating to attention and understanding are applied. There is no need to adhere doggedly to the detail of a particular session plan if it is inappropriate for any reason – for example, if children have particular anxieties or obsessions, or if resource materials are unavailable.

Part I

3 to 5 year-olds

Social Skills Programmes

Setting the Scene

CRITERIA FOR ADMISSION

- Child's attention level is at Stage 3 (will attend to adult's choice of activity, but may be difficult to control) (Cooper, Moodley & Reynell, 1978).

- Comprehension is at the level of three information-carrying words.

- The child will have been identified as having social communication problems, which may or may not have been diagnosed as an autistic spectrum disorder.

- There is no cognitive disability.

- The child's range of difficulties is qualitatively different from a straightforward language delay/disorder.

- There is language present, but it is not used communicatively. There may be a derived or learnt quality in the child's expression.

- There are no serious behaviour problems.

- The child can separate or learn easily to separate from his parent.

THE PROGRAMME

At this level we suggest you run 10 sessions, preceded by a parents' workshop, and followed by individual parent interviews. *The involvement of parents is vital.*

It is more likely that a programme for children aged 3 to 5 years will be run by the speech and language therapy service. The reason for this is the necessity of close involvement of the mother or carer in a way that is particular to this age group. For this reason, the programme is set out with the assumption that it will take place in a health centre or clinic. However, everything included in the programme can be adapted and used just as well in a nursery or playgroup setting.

The first two sessions can be run on a 'trial' basis; some children may have to be excluded as group needs have to be paramount.

AIMS

- Sitting
- Looking
- Listening
- Turn-taking

These skills have to be established. They are the skills that underpin access to learning and social interaction.

PRACTICALITIES

Time:	One to one-and-a-half hours.
Size of group:	For ages 3 to 5 years, it is advisable to have no more than six children.
Staffing:	Two speech & language therapists (SLTs), or one SLT and an assistant, and one parent helper on a rota basis.
Finance:	Petty cash to cover snack-time drinks and biscuits, and incidental expenses.
	Ask for weekly contributions to a piggy bank for a final session party. Decide in advance what is an appropriate amount, and get agreement from parents at the workshop session.
Equipment:	Time-Line.
	Timetable.
	Paired pictures/labels.
	Box or bag to collect items children bring in.
	Bags for games.
	Rope with knots.
	Cassette/CD player and recordings of action songs or rhymes for young children.
	Name labels.
	Homework record notebooks (for parents' use).
Snacks:	Drinks (two kinds), biscuits, cups, tray, apron, jug, plate, helpers' list.
Shared play:	Short play sessions with an emphasis on sharing and turn-taking may be incorporated. It is up to the professionals running the group to decide how and when to do this. A play session may be substituted for an activity, or added as an extra if and when time allows. Items of equipment such as marble runs or train sets that require some construction are particularly useful for this purpose.

Parents' Workshop

This format can be used for all groups, but may need adaptation in relation to older children.

1 Tea/coffee and introductions.

2 Reminders of dates of group sessions.

3 Explain arrangements for parent interviews after the final group session.

4 Explain if and when contact will be made with schools or nurseries.

5 Attendance: Explain that attendance at all sessions is vital, as is good timekeeping.

6 Discuss the parents' role in completing homework tasks.

7 Remind parents to talk about the group at home in the week between sessions. Show the time-line or individual calendar, if relevant.

8 Discuss snack time and the rules that will apply (see Session 1). Ask for information about any allergies.

9 Discuss any arrangements for parents to attend the group sessions on a rota basis.

10 Provide written information about homework tasks.

11 Advise parents when reports about children's progress will be sent and circulated.

12 Discuss possible follow-up arrangements when the group ends.

13 Discuss particular concerns of individual parents, and what they hope their child will achieve.

14 Advise parents that the first two sessions are a trial period for all participants. If a child does not settle for any reason, it may be better for everyone if he ceases to attend, with the expectation that another group will be offered at a later date.

Settling Down

SESSION 1

1. Meet the children and their parents in the waiting room. Collect money for the piggy bank.

2. Ask the children to hold on to knots in the rope. The group leader encourages everyone to say, 'Goodbye, see you soon' to their parents. This can be in the form of a song for the musically inclined! (The Nordoff-Robbins music therapy programme includes suitable songs for such situations.)

3. Ask the children to sit in a circle, on chairs labelled with their names. They can then choose a picture sticker to go with their name. Introduce the idea of 'good sitting', with a demonstration.

4. Play the 'Hello' game. This consists of the group leader saying 'Hello' and the child's name to one child, who has to return the greeting and give eye contact. The group leader then asks that child, 'Who would you like to say hello to?' The game continues until all the children have had a turn. A 'hello' song can be used to reinforce this with young children.

5. Pass a toy to the next child in the circle, using his name. Reinforce this with 'Who will you pass the toy to?'

6. *Snack Time*. The table and chairs will need to be reorganised. A child helper is then appointed who wears a special apron and ticks his name on a list to register his turn. His role includes counting the number of cups needed; asking the other children what they would like to drink, and offering biscuits. The purpose of snack time is to encourage the children to make choices, take turns, wait, use 'please' and 'thank you', and to make eye contact. They will also learn some organisational skills; to cooperate when clearing away, and how to reform the circle once snack time is over.

Some simple rules for snack time need to be explained:

- Children can choose from just two sorts of drink. (In the first few sessions, pointing can be accepted.)

- If no choice is made, the helper is encouraged to ask the next child, and should only return to the first child when everyone else has been served.

SESSION 1

- It is easier to provide only one kind of biscuit for this age group, and when they are offered on a plate, only one should be touched and taken.

- There should be no eating or drinking until the whole group has been served. The point of this is to encourage awareness of the needs of others. If children find this difficult, the drinks can be placed on a tray to discourage grabbing and make the waiting easier.

7 *Singalong* to a tape.

8 *Time-Line.* Explain this to the group and fill it in.
The time-line consists of a long strip of heavy-duty paper or card, marked out with days of the week, for the period of the group. Group days are highlighted in some way, by a colour or a small sticker perhaps. A small cut-out picture of a car or an animal, or something else the children like, should be used to move along the time-line so that they understand the sequence of the weekly sessions.

9 Return to the waiting room with the knotted rope.

10 *Homework:* Hand out the Parent Sheet. Parents are also provided with a list of the children's names to discuss at home, with questions such as who is a boy or girl; who did their child sit next to; who was the helper? A photograph of the group leaders can be given. Parents are asked to help their child find a photograph of himself, which will be displayed for the duration of the group.

SHEET FOR PARENTS

Settling Down

SESSION 1

Certain core activities will feature in each group session. These will include:

- Meeting, greeting and separating.
- Self-organisation in relation to other children in the group.
- Using a visual timetable to anticipate activities.
- Snack time, when children will learn about requesting, choosing and turn-taking.
- Using a time-line to anticipate and think ahead to the next group session.
- Homework tasks to reinforce the focus of each session.
- Revision/recall of the focus of the previous session.

This first session aims to develop self-awareness, awareness of others, and making choices. The children have been introduced to the importance of attending through good sitting. (Looking, listening and turn-taking will feature in later sessions.)

HOMEWORK

Use the list of children's names to talk about the session at home. Ask questions such as, who is a boy or girl; who did your child sit next to; what happened at snack time? Talk about the adults running the group. Help your child find a photograph of himself to bring to the next session. Photographs will be displayed for the duration of the group.

Since the ability to sit reasonably still is a prerequisite for the development of attention skills, it is important to encourage your child to do this when appropriate. The term 'good sitting' can be used both as a standard to be aimed at, and as a positive reinforcement. This is preferable to comments such as 'sit still', 'don't fidget', or 'stop kicking'.

Please ensure that you arrive in good time to collect your child, and to be advised about homework tasks.

Please fill in the weekly record of your child's responses to the homework task in the notebook. Feel free to add any comments that you feel are relevant and helpful.

SESSION 2 — What Happens Next?

1 Meet up in the waiting room. Collect money for the piggy bank.

2 Ask the children to hold a knot in the rope; sing the 'Goodbye' song to their parents, and say 'See you soon'.

3 Ask the children to find the seat with their label and sticker. (The chairs have already been arranged in a circle.) Remind them about 'good sitting'.

4 Play the 'Hello' game plus a song.

5 Look at the photographs and put them on display. Talk about differences between the children – eye/skin colour, gender, hair length, clothes, and so on.

6 Introduce the timetable. Choose a child to select the first activity.

7 Play a turn-taking game. The chosen child selects one item from a box of small toys of intrinsic interest that are easy to handle – for example, snow scenes, wind-up toys, or spinning items. Everyone has a turn with it. The group leader reinforces the concept of turn-taking by frequent use of 'Whose turn is it now?' … 'It's Tom's turn now.'

8 Choose another child to select a second activity. (This system of selection of the next activity is thus established for all future sessions.)

9 Look at a book or simple story.

10 *Snack Time*. Follow the same routine as in the first session. This will continue for all subsequent sessions.

11 Sing along to a tape.

12 *Time-Line*. Ask a child to move the picture along.

13 Return to the waiting room with the rope. (This may continue for all sessions or can be varied as suggested later.)

14 *Homework*: The children are to bring something from the bathroom next time. Ask parents to continue to discuss the group, referring to group members and using their names. Give all parents a copy of the Parent Sheet.

SHEET FOR PARENTS

What Happens Next?

SESSION 2

The focus for this session was **anticipation.** To encourage children to think about 'what happens next', a visual timetable has been introduced. This will enable them to see beyond the immediate, and to develop an awareness of events as a sequence. The time-line at the end of each session will also reinforce this concept.

The children have been encouraged to think about each other; what they look like, and what they are wearing. The idea of turn-taking has been introduced through the use of toys and simple games.

HOMEWORK

You should continue to talk about the group, using the names of individuals.

It will also be helpful to reinforce the concept of anticipation by talking about forthcoming events affecting the child, such as outings, seeing relatives, or birthdays.

It is important to involve your child or inform him of changes that are about to take place. For example, a family member going into hospital; getting a new or different job; even moving house. Children are likely to cope better if they are given simple explanations that are regularly reinforced.

Please help your child to choose an item from the bathroom to show and talk about at the next group session.

SESSION 3

Talk About

1 Meet in the waiting room. Collect money for the piggy bank.

2 Ask the children to hold a knot in the rope; sing 'Goodbye' to their parents, and say 'see you soon'.

3 The children find the seat with their own label and sticker. The chairs are already set out.

4 Play the 'Hello' game, as before.

5 Homework topic (items from bathroom). Identify the objects and who they belong to; then put them out on a tray for later on. (Group leaders may need to bring in some items too.)

6 Timetable. Revise what it means. A child selects the first activity, as before.

7 Topic work – bathrooms. Discuss the items – their function, shape, colour, and so on.

8 *Snack Time*, as before.

9 Singing. Include actions and miming of bathroom activities. For example, 'This is the way we brush our hair'.

10 *Time-Line*, as before.

11 Return to the waiting room **holding hands**, not with the rope.

12 *Homework*: Ask the parents to talk to the children about bathrooms, and to bring in something from the garden or park for next week. Hand out the Parent Sheet.

SHEET FOR PARENTS

Talk About

SESSION 3

The focus for this session was **keeping to topic** and **providing information**. The theme was bathrooms. The children had to name the item they brought, and to talk about its function, shape and colour. They were encouraged to add as much information as possible, including concepts such as texture or ownership, as relevant.

The children were encouraged to join in singing and action songs. This reinforced the idea of working together with others in a group and not opting out.

HOMEWORK

You should discuss bathrooms, as it was this week's topic. Talk about what goes on in the bathroom. Talk about why we wash. Where does the dirty water go? Ensure that the child stays on topic. If he veers away from the topic and introduces irrelevancies, simply say 'We are not talking about that now', and ask the child to recall what was being discussed.

Please help your child to select an item from the garden or park to bring to the next session.

SESSION 4

Good Looking

1 Meet in the waiting room. Collect money for the piggy bank.

2 All hold hands to walk to the room.

3 Children find their own seats, as before.

4 Play the 'Hello' game followed by 'You're looking at me'. One of the adults hides their eyes behind their hands, then looks up directly at one particular child, using their hands as blinkers. The child acknowledges this by saying 'You're looking at me'. The game continues until each child has been 'looked at'. It may be possible for the children to take the lead in this game.

5 Timetable.

6 Turn-taking activity. The chosen child selects one item from a box of small toys of intrinsic interest that are easy to handle – for example, snow scenes, wind-up toys, or spinning items. Everyone has a turn with it. The group leader reinforces the concept of turn-taking by frequent use of 'Whose turn is it now?' ... 'It's Tom's turn now.'

7 Homework topic – talk about gardens and parks.

8 *Snack Time.*

9 Play a game of 'Who's sitting on the big chair?' One big chair is placed at a point in a circle of small chairs. The children walk around the chairs singing 'Ring-a-ring-a-roses' – ending with the line 'We all sit down'. One child gets the big chair. The adult asks, 'Who's sitting on the big chair?' The children all point and name the child. Every child gets a turn to land on the big chair.

10 *Time-Line.*

11 Return to the waiting room **holding hands**.

12 *Homework*: Drawing eyes for 'good looking'. Parents reinforce this by talking to the child about eyes and eye colour, and getting the child to give eye contact on request. Hand out the Parent Sheet.

SHEET FOR PARENTS

Good Looking

SESSION 4

The majority of children attending the group will have difficulty with eye contact, to a greater or lesser extent. The aim of this session was to promote **good looking**. This was facilitated through games and activities in which eye contact is an essential aspect. In other words, if a child is not looking properly he will be unable to join in.

We then talked about gardens and parks, which enhanced the children's vocabulary and reinforced the concept of relevance.

HOMEWORK

At home reinforce the importance of good eye contact. The term 'good looking' is a useful trigger to encourage appropriate visual contact. It is better to familiarise the child with this format than to use variable or possibly confusing reminders such as 'You're not looking at me', or 'Why don't you look at me?'

Draw eyes with your child to build awareness of 'good looking'. Talk to your child about eyes, eye colour, glasses, and so on. Take the pictures with you to the next session.

SESSION 5

In, On, Under

1 Meet in the waiting room. Collect money for the piggy bank.

2 Walk to the room in a line like a snake, with hands on the shoulders of the child in front.

3 Sit in a circle, as before.

4 Play the 'Hello' game, as before.

5 Timetable.

6 Topic work – eyes. Ask all the children to show their homework. Then turn this into an activity where the children colour in each others' eye pictures, using traced outlines or photocopies.

7 Introduce three basic prepositions (**in**, **on**, **under**) with a box and a toy. Reinforce these using signs (Paget-Gorman signs are particularly useful).

8 *Snack Time.*

9 Play a game of 'Old MacDonald'. Put a range of farm animals into a bag. Each child in turn picks an animal from the bag at the appropriate point in the song.

10 *Time-Line.*

11 Return to the waiting room in a line with **no touching**.

12 *Homework*: Ask the children to bring in a favourite soft toy, such as a teddy bear. Hand out the Parent Sheet.

SHEET FOR PARENTS

In, On, Under

SESSION 5

A surprisingly large number of able children with social communication difficulties, and learnt rather than self-generated language, show little awareness of the distinctions between **on**, **in** and **under**. They may understand them in some familiar contexts, but not in others. For example, the child may respond easily to the instruction 'Put the book **on** the table', because books are *always* put on the table. However, he may also do this when told to put the book **under** the table. In other words, the understanding of **under** has not been extended beyond a particular situation. It shows that the child has not really understood its meaning.

This session focused on the use of these prepositions (position words) in a variety of ways, which included manual signs, objects and body positions. It is not unusual for a child to understand position words in relation to objects, but not to his own body.

This topic will be developed further in Sessions 7 and 8.

HOMEWORK

Reinforce your child's understanding of **in**, **on** and **under** in your everyday activities at home or at the shops.

For next week, encourage your child to bring in his favourite soft toy.

SESSION 6
Good Listening

1 Meet in the waiting room. Collect money for the piggy bank.

2 Ask the children to walk to the room in a line, without any touching.

3 Play the 'Hello' game.

4 Timetable.

5 Ask the children to sit and listen to some classical music (for one to two minutes only). Encourage quietness and sitting still.

6 Homework topic. The children take turns to show their toys, say something about them and pass them around the group.

7 Use their toys for revision of **in**, **on** and **under.**

8 *Snack Time.*

9 Play a 'listening to instructions' game called 'In the Sack'. A range of objects or pictures is set out on a table. Each child is called by name to put at least two objects or pictures into the sack. Increase the number of objects or pictures for good listeners.

10 *Time-Line.*

11 Return to the waiting room in a line, with children in order of height.

12 *Homework*: Ask the cildren to bring in two items of clothing – one for hot weather, and one for cold. Make sure everybody picks up a Parent Sheet.

SHEET FOR PARENTS

Good Listening

SESSION 6

The majority of children in the group will have poor **listening skills** and will benefit from specific input in this area. This is apparent even in those with relatively well-developed expressive language. Indeed, it is easy to be beguiled by a child who can expound at some length on a topic of interest with a repertoire of appropriate, but nevertheless learnt phrases and associative comments. **Echolalia** is often a feature of poor listening: this is where the child repeats the words he hears, but does not comprehend the underlying meaning.

In this session, the children were introduced to focused listening. This will be continued in future sessions. Since most children generally respond positively to music, the session included a few minutes at the outset when they were expected to sit and listen to a short extract of classical music. This practice has been found to be helpful in establishing an atmosphere of calm and readiness for the rest of the session. Sometimes children arrive for the group in a state of stress because of an earlier upset. The music provides a marker that enables them to set aside these upsets and participate fully in the group's activities.

The session also included activities that involved listening to detailed instructions and responding appropriately.

Another focus for this session was **sharing**. By bringing in a favourite toy, which was shown and passed around the group, the children are learning the meaning of turn-taking and sharing. They were also encouraged to talk about their own toy, and to develop some awareness of the needs and interests of others.

HOMEWORK

Talk to your child about his and your favourite things, and the likes and dislikes of others. When opportunities arise in play situations, remind your child about taking turns and sharing.

For next week, please bring in two items of your child's clothing – one for hot weather and one for winter.

  This page may be photocopied for instructional use only. *Social Skills Programmes* © M Aarons & T Gittens 2003

SESSION 7 — In front of, Behind, Next to

1 Meet in the waiting room. Collect money for the piggy bank.

2 Walk to the room in a line according to height (the reverse from last week).

3 Play the 'Hello' game.

4 Timetable.

5 Sit in a circle to listen to music, as before.

6 Homework topic. The children subdivide the items of clothing into the categories 'hot' and 'cold', and place them in two boxes with appropriate logos. Adults 'model' how to do this with their items of clothing. The clothes should then be further subdivided into those suitable for boys and the ones that are best for girls. Do any fit both categories? Use more boxes.

7 Work on prepositions. Introduce **in front of**, **behind**, **next to.**

8 Play a preposition game. Children listen in turn to an instruction, and place themselves in an appropriate position relative to a large object – for example, a chair or a table.

9 *Snack Time*.

10 *Story Time*. Read an appropriate story to the group to reinforce prepositions, such as *We're Going on a Bear Hunt*, or *He's Behind You*.

11 *Time-Line*.

12 Return to the waiting room. The group leader picks a child who has done some good work to lead the line.

13 *Homework*: Ask the children to bring in their favourite soft toy again next week. Give all parents the Parent Sheet for Session 7.

SHEET FOR PARENTS

In front of, Behind, Next to [SESSION 7]

The term 'weak central coherence' has been used to pinpoint the difficulty inherent in children with autistic spectrum disorders. They have difficulty appreciating what is meaningful to enable them to make sense of the world. This may be relevant to your child's understanding. The purpose of this session was to encourage the children to begin to **classify** and **categorise**. Using the items of clothing, they had to think about which ones keep you warm; which ones are for hot days; which are for boys, and which are for girls. In other words, they were required to start thinking about things that go beyond the 'here and now'. This activity marked the beginning of an ongoing process of learning, which is vital for all children with social communication difficulties.

HOMEWORK

In this session we have talked about **in front of**, **behind** and **next to**. Please reinforce these positions during the week. You can use toys or objects around the house (such as a chair, an armchair, settee or curtains), and ask your child to stand in one or other of the three positions in relation to them. Next week we will focus on position words (prepositions) in greater detail.

For next week, please ask your child to bring in a favourite soft toy again.

| SESSION 8 | # Think About Position |

1 Meet in the waiting room. Collect money for the piggy bank.

2 Walk to the room like a line of marching soldiers. (The group leader models what is required.)

3 Play the 'Hello' game.

4 Timetable.

5 Sit in a circle to listen to music, as before.

6 Homework topic. Reintroduce the soft toys. Who can remember who they belong to, and any other details? Children take it in turns to place their toy **on** the floor and stand **in front of**, **behind** or **next to** it. **On**, **in** and **under** should also be revised.

7 Read an appropriate story with the group, such as *Each Peach Pear Plum*, to reinforce prepositions.

8 *Snack Time*. Ask the children who they would like to sit **next to**, or who they are already sitting **next to**.

9 Play 'Simon Says', reinforcing prepositions.

10 *Time-Line*.

11 Return to the waiting room in a line. Ask the children to stand **in front of** or **behind** others in the group.

12 *Homework*: The children are asked to bring in a picture about their favourite television programme. They can draw this, or bring in a toy or book based on the programme – a Teletubby or a Barney the Dinosaur, for example. Hand out the Parent Sheet as a reminder.

SHEET FOR PARENTS

Think About Position

SESSION 8

In this session we reinforce the work done on position in previous sessions.

The understanding of prepositions (position words) is very often dependent on the context, and many children need a substantial amount of help to be able to appreciate their meaning. It is very easy to assume understanding because, typically, they will use phrases such as '**on** the table', or '**in** the bath', but fail to respond appropriately to instructions or requests using such prepositions in a more specific way. It is only when the child is asked to place an object **on**, **in**, **under**, **by**, **next to**, **in front of**, or **behind** another object that he reveals his lack of understanding. Some children seem disinclined to use prepositions at all, and will point or simply respond 'there'. This may be because they expect the adult to know what they mean and are therefore not aware of the necessity to give precise information about the location of an object. We have worked on these prepositions in the session today.

HOMEWORK

You can improve your child's understanding and use of position words every day. You can do this in relation to daily routines such as laying the table, tidying up, getting ready for bed, and playing in the bath. To ensure that your child really understands, introduce games that involve putting things in unexpected places. For example, a hat **under** a plate, pyjamas **behind** a chair, an apple **on** the television set.

For next week, please help your child to find a picture, or draw a picture, to show a favourite television programme. Alternatively, your child can bring in a toy or book based on the programme, such as a Teletubby or Barney the Dinosaur.

| SESSION 9 | # Likes & Dislikes |

1 Meet in the waiting room. Collect money for the piggy bank.

2 Walk to the room in a line after instructions to stand **behind** or **in front of** each other.

3 Play the 'Hello' game.

4 Timetable.

5 Sit in a circle to listen to music, as before.

6 Homework topic. Take turns to talk about favourite television programmes. A cardboard box with a hole representing the screen, with a transparent A4 pocket into which the children can slide their pictures, makes this activity very appealing. Remind children about the session when favourite toys were brought in. Ask everyone what their favourite colour is. A chart could be drawn to illustrate likes and dislikes.

7 The piggy bank is opened and the money counted. Talk about next week's party, and ask everyone to say what they would like to eat.

8 *Snack Time*.

9 Talk about the party; what to wear; what games to play, and so on.

10 All join in some action songs using early years' tapes – for example, 'Heads, shoulders, knees and toes'.

11 *Time-Line*. Link this to anticipating next week's party, and reinforcing the message that it will be the last group session.

12 *Homework*: Ask the children to make a hat to wear at the party. Make sure all parents leave with a Parent Sheet.

SHEET FOR PARENTS

Likes & Dislikes

SESSION 9

In this session we focused on **personal preferences**, encouraging the children to think beyond their favourite toy to such things as colour and food. The latter links into next week's party. Extend this topic by talking about family members' likes and dislikes. The family pet's preferences can also be talked about. If your child is rigid about likes and dislikes, this may help towards a degree of flexibility. A simple wall chart may spark an interest in trying new things.

HOMEWORK

Next week is the final group session. Using the money you have contributed to the piggy bank, we shall be having a party. Help your child make a simple hat or crown to wear at the party.

SESSION 10 — Saying Goodbye

1 Meet in the waiting room.

2 Ask the children to walk to the room, holding hands.

3 Play the 'Hello' game for the final time.

4 Timetable.

5 Homework topic. Discuss the party: what has been brought in; the food bought with the piggy bank money, and so on.

6 *Activity*. The children select particular items of food and put them on plates. Discuss preferences, taste, appearance, and so on at the same time.

7 Play party games such as 'Musical bumps' and 'Pass the parcel', with small sweets as prizes. 'The farmer's in his den' is another good game.

8 Party-food time – snack time rules apply.

9 *Time-Line*. Remind children that this is the last session.

10 Say goodbye with a song.

11 The children collect their parents, and bring them to the room for more goodbyes. Give out evaluation forms, and organise follow-up appointments for parents. Tell them that written reports on each child's progress will follow.

SHEET FOR PARENTS

Saying Goodbye

SESSION 10

This final session was a celebration to mark the end of the group. May we suggest that if your child has shown a liking for, or even an interest in any other child or children, that you get together with the parents to build on the relationship.

Please continue to reinforce the work you have been doing with your child, particularly in relation to sitting, looking, listening and turn-taking.

Please remember to talk to your child about things that are happening in the family. Episodes of difficult behaviour are often linked to events in the home that the child does not understand. Never assume that he has understood a situation simply on the basis of given information. For example, you may have told your child you are moving to a new house, but he may not realise that he will not be returning to the old one. You tell him 'Mummy has a job and will be going out to work', but how is he to understand that you will be back every evening? Be aware that his style of thinking is very concrete and lacking in flexibility, so that he may not draw the conclusions that you expect.

Please remember to complete the evaluation form, and to make an appointment to discuss your child's progress. Following this, you will receive a written report.

In about six months' time, your child's progress will be reviewed and you will be asked to complete a further evaluation form. This will help to determine whether your child might benefit from a further social skills group.

This page may be photocopied for instructional use only. *Social Skills Programmes* © M Aarons & T Gittens 2003

Part II

5 to 7 year-olds

Setting the Scene

CRITERIA FOR ADMISSION

Refer to the early years (ages 3 to 5) programme (page 2) for general principles.

LINKING WITH EDUCATION

At this level, children will be in a variety of educational settings, which will affect the nature of the groups and the ways in which they are organised. These may include special schools and units, as well as mainstream primary schools. Although, ideally, social skills groups should be an educational provision, this is not always feasible – for a variety of reasons. For example, a single mainstream school may not have sufficient numbers of suitable children to form a viable group, or groups. In such circumstances, a clinic or health centre may continue to be the most suitable location, and therefore the provision of social skills groups will remain the responsibility of the speech and language therapy service. This should not preclude the Local Education Authority (LEA in the UK) from contributing financially to such provision. Children can be brought together from a number of different schools, thereby ensuring a good mix of suitable children. If this is the arrangement, every effort should be made for each child's teacher to attend at least one session of the series, and to have an opportunity at the outset to discuss the child's most pressing needs with the speech & language therapist (SLT). This should be with the agreement of the parents.

It also makes sense to provide teachers as well as parents with any relevant information about the group – for example, homework tasks. Ideally, there should be a team approach involving the speech & language therapists, class teachers, support staff and special educational needs coordinators (SENCOs). This is not always easy when the group sessions take place outside school premises. Inset training by the SLT in the different schools involved is a way of fostering relationships and cooperation. In any case, a workshop session for all the teachers involved is essential (see page 31) so that they are aware not only of the overall aims, but the content of the sessions and the resources that will be used. Increasingly, in the UK – and possibly resulting from inclusion policies – LEAs are now employing SLTs, not only in special schools, but in mainstream settings too. This is in accordance with growing awareness that children's communication difficulties are intrinsically linked to their educational needs and their ability to access the curriculum.

The introduction of both literacy and numeracy hours into the national curriculum in the UK has had an impact on access to children by visiting professionals, including SLTs, during school hours. In addition, the demands of the national curriculum mean that there is very little time when children can be withdrawn on a regular basis. The only practical solution may be to run the groups outside school hours, or towards the end of the school day.

AIMS

Before embarking on the 5 to 7 years programme, it is essential that the aims of the early years (3 to 5) programme have been accomplished. This means that the children should be able to sit, look, listen, and show some understanding of turn-taking for the duration of group sessions. It does not mean that they will necessarily be able to maintain this without reminders. Children aged from 5 to 7 years with learning difficulties may need to revise the early years' skills before moving on to this programme.

The aims at this level are the **consolidation of the above skills** into everyday situations that are meaningful and relevant to the children. It is important that parents and teachers make the same demands on children in terms of standards of behaviour and compliance as are achieved in the group setting.

Children need to be made aware that skills introduced in the group can, and should, be transferred to other situations. They are not just for practising once a week in the social skills session.

Inevitably, some children will have difficulty keeping still, which is why it is important to continue to use music at the start of each session as a trigger for 'good sitting'. At this level, the children should be able to contrast this with 'fidgeting'. It helps to actually practise fidgeting, which can then be physically experienced and compared with sitting still without moving about. If this is attempted at an earlier developmental stage, the children may become over excited and difficult to control.

PRACTICALITIES

It is up to the person organising the group to decide whether or not to use the suggestions made for the 3 to 5 years group (see page 3). Much will depend on the maturity of the children, which will also affect the size of the group. It may be possible to increase the number of children from six to eight if they are generally compliant.

It is unlikely that a rope with knots, for example, will be needed to move children around. However, they will certainly still require a visual timetable and time-line to reinforce the idea of 'what happens next'. There is a tendency for adults to do too much for children, particularly those who find it difficult to organise themselves when time is short. For this reason, getting the children to arrange their chairs at the beginning and end of each session is an important aspect of thinking for themselves, in a situation when the needs of others have to be considered. It is often quite illuminating to observe the range of difficulties that this seemingly simple task throws up. Some children stand around waiting for things to happen; others tell everyone else what to do and over organise, while some show such passivity that they seem to be unaware that they have been relegated to a position outside the circle.

Children should be provided with a personalised transparent plastic pocket, in which they can keep homework, worksheets, badges and so on, which they bring to each session. The pockets will serve as a focus to remind the children of their group, and what they have to think about. At the final session, it may be a good idea to give a certificate, badge or sticker to each child as a reward for attendance and effort. (See page 161.)

At the parents' workshop, remind them of their role in helping their child with simple homework tasks about which they will be briefed at the end of each session, or contacted via a home/school notebook. These books will be useful in other ways. For example, they can provide the group leader with information about children's out-of-school activities to talk about at news time (Session 3 onwards).

Children with social communication problems have difficulty appreciating that other people do not necessarily know what they know. This becomes most obvious when they are required to provide information or explanations. They assume the listener knows everything they know, and have to be taught to think about what other people may or may not know.

Teachers' Workshop

(FOR CHILDREN AGED 5 TO 11 YEARS)

- Flexibility is essential, since teachers will have varying degrees of experience of working with children with social communication problems, as well as those with special educational needs. The workshop could be run as a formal Inset session, or on informal lines with familiar colleagues. Obviously depending on the context of the workshop, the content will have to be adapted according to what is relevant.

- At the outset, it will be necessary to clarify the roles of those who are to be involved with running the groups; these will have to be negotiated to ensure consistency.

- Describe and discuss the sort of children who are likely to benefit from social skills groups. Include a discussion of diagnostic issues as relevant.

- Discuss the rationale for a social skills approach.

- Introduce the social skills programmes and discuss their content.

- Demonstrate the time-line, and visual aids such as session timetables, work folders and books.

- Discuss the role of parents and the ways in which they can be involved, especially in relation to weekly homework tasks. Talk about such options as a home/school notebook, or an information sheet for distribution each week. (These could be prepared on similar lines to those used in the 3 to 5 years' programme.) It should be borne in mind that talking to individual parents each week is unlikely to be practical, unless a serious problem arises and needs to be discussed. (Emphasise that parents of school-aged children will have a workshop session before the start of a group, and an individual interview at the end.)

SESSION 1

Observation & Awareness of Others

1 Chairs are arranged in a circle. The children are made aware of this in readiness for doing it themselves next week.

2 A short extract of classical music is played, and the children are required to sit still and listen without fidgeting. Inevitably, some children will fidget. The difference between fidgeting and sitting still can be demonstrated at this stage.

3 Introduce everybody and ask them all to make name badges.

4 Play a game to learn and remember everyone's name. All name badges (for children and adults) are put in a bag, which is passed around. Each child selects a badge and identifies its owner.

5 'Why are we here?' Explain to the group, in very general terms, that everyone needs to learn how to sit and not fidget; how to listen and not interrupt, and how to take turns and be good friends. A poster can be made listing these aims, on which the children can draw themselves or write their names.

6 Activity. 'What Do We Look Like?' The children are called in turn to stand by an adult. The other children are asked to identify particular details – boy/girl, hair colour, clothes, and so on. After all the children have had a turn, the game 'Who am I talking about?' is introduced. (The adult describes a child for others to identify.)

7 *Snack time.* (See page 5). The childrens' names are listed, and one is selected to be the server. Explain that a different child will be chosen from the list each week, so that everyone will have turn.

8 Introduce 'Harry' showing good sitting, and give out Harry posters.

9 Talk about homework.

10 *Time-Line.*

11 The children are asked to put away chairs and line up, and give eye contact to say goodbye. This may have to be practised over the coming weeks.

12 *Homework*: Ask the children to colour in the Harry poster, and to bring in a photo or drawing of themselves for next week.

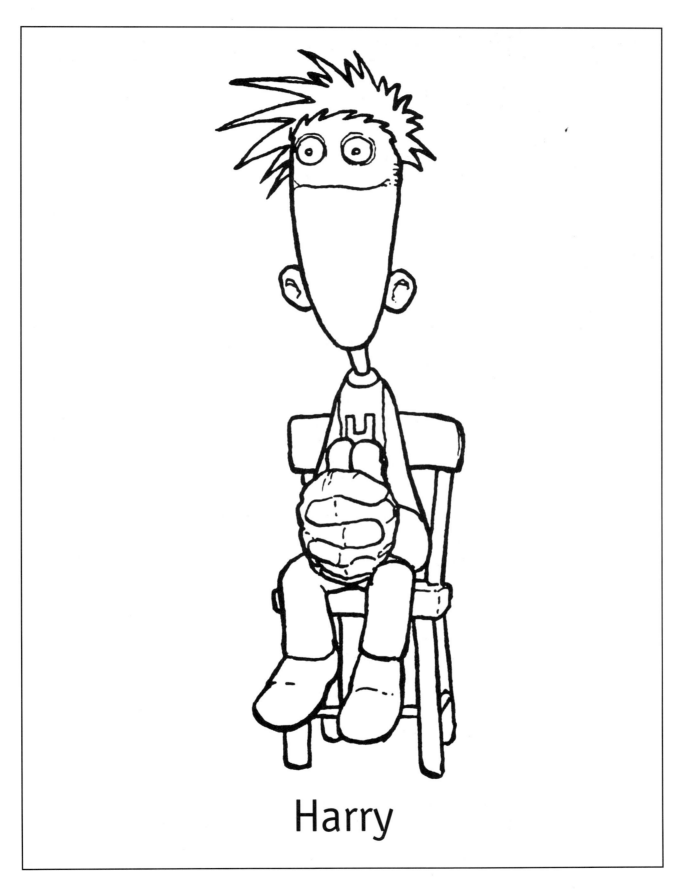

HARRY'S STORY

Aim of the story: To highlight fidgeting as opposed to good sitting.

1 Harry and Charlie are sitting in a group listening to a story.

2 Charlie is sitting very still.

3 Harry is rocking on his chair and distracting other children by touching them.

4 Suddenly Harry falls off his chair and hurts his head, and cries.

5 The children are fed up because they cannot hear the story.

6 Charlie shows Harry how to sit properly like all the other children.

Good Looking

SESSION 2

1 Ask the children to put out the chairs. (They may be helped by a marked or drawn circle on the floor.)

2 Ask for good sitting while music is being played, as before.

3 Play the 'Hello' game (see page 5).

4 Look at the homework tasks. Make a display poster using the photos or drawings that have been brought in. Photos or drawings of the adults should be included.

5 Molly's story. Give out posters to colour in for homework.

6 Play the 'Looking for Molly' game. One child leaves the room with an adult, and returns with a small 'Molly' logo stuck any part of their visible clothing or body – shoe, elbow, collar, and so on. Other children have to spot 'Molly' and say where it is. Everyone has a turn.

7 *Snack Time*. Another child is chosen from the list. The emphasis is on looking. Every child has to look at the server when they make their choice, and maintain eye contact to say thank you.

8 Play the game 'Passing the gesture'. To play this, an adult starts the game by making one clear gesture – waving a hand, crossing legs, yawning, scratching their nose, and so on, and the gesture is passed around the circle. The last child starts the game again with a different gesture.

9 Talk about the homework.

10 *Time-Line*.

11 Everybody helps to put the chairs away and line up, as in Session 1.

12 *Homework*: Colour in 'Molly' poster. Everyone must do some special 'good looking' and tell us about it next week. For example, looking at Granny, baby brother or sister, the family pet, and thereby being able to respond to simple questions such as, 'What colour is Granny's hair?', or 'Does your baby walk?'

Molly

MOLLY'S STORY

Aim of the story: To develop understanding of the importance of looking at others to facilitate communication.

1 Charlie meets Molly and wants to tell her his news.

2 Molly does not look at him when he talks to her. She looks at other things.

3 Charlie feels upset. He thinks she is not interested in his news.

4 Charlie explains why Molly has to look at other people when talking together.

5 Molly says she is sorry and will remember that and try harder.

6 Molly is now better at making friends and gets on better in school.

SESSION 3 — Good Listening

1 Ask the children to arrange the chairs, giving them minimal direction.

2 Good sitting with music, as before.

3 Play the 'Hello' game, as before.

4 Follow up last week's homework tasks on 'good looking'.

5 Read the 'Florrie' story. Give out the posters for homework.

6 Introduce 'giving news'. An adult models this by giving a piece of information about a recent experience, for example: 'On Saturday I went to see a film'. Some children will find this very difficult. The use of a group/home diary or notebook will enable the adult to cue in those who need help. Ensure that the child is made aware of who gave the information. For example, 'Your mummy told me that your granny came to stay'.

7 Carry out a group activity for sharing toys. A small selection of interesting toys that move, wind up or whirr are offered. Each child chooses a toy and has a chance to play with it, before passing it on to the next child.

8 *Snack Time.* As before, emphasise the importance of listening as well as looking. The group leader can reinforce this by asking the server to repeat each child's request.

9 The children are asked to listen to a story. (Choose a story where there are opportunities for the children to join in – the big books used for literacy hour are ideal in terms of their visual appeal.)

10 *Time-Line.*

11 The children put away the chairs and check if the room is tidy before lining up, as before.

12 *Homework:* Colour in the 'Florrie' poster. Think about today's story to talk about next week. Think of some news to tell next week. Parents or teachers may need to assist children in deciding on a news topic.

Florrie

FLORRIE'S STORY

Aim of the story: To demonstrate the importance of listening and why it is not good to interrupt.

1 At playtime, Florrie is telling her friends about her trip to the seaside.

2 Dennis is not listening and interrupts Florrie to talk about his trip to the park.

3 The friends are cross. They are listening and want to hear the rest of Florrie's news.

4 Florrie tells Dennis to wait and listen and then he can tell his news.

5 Dennis says he is sorry, he did not think.

6 Dennis tells his news when Florrie has finished telling hers.

Turn-Taking

SESSION 4

1 The children put out the chairs without any help, if possible.

2 Good sitting time, with music.

3 Play the 'Hello' game.

4 Giving news.

5 Follow-up of homework: recall of last week's story. Who were the characters? What was the story about? What happened at the end?, and so on.

6 Read the 'Boris and Bertie' story. Give out the posters for homework.

7 Carry out turn-taking with toys, as before. It may emerge that some children have particular difficulty in understanding turn-taking. It may be helpful to introduce a specific activity to demonstrate what it is about. With children sitting in a circle, the group leader points to each child in turn saying, 'Your turn now', indicating that they should copy her action of raising and lowering an arm. This very simple activity usually suffices.

8 *Snack Time*. Give reminders about turn-taking, emphasising that it should be applied to different situations. Discuss what these situations might be.

9 *Time-Line*.

10 Put away the chairs and line up.

11 *Homework*: Colour in the 'Boris and Bertie' poster. Turn-taking is to be reinforced both at home and in school, with frequent reminders. Everyone must bring in a toy to the next session to show and share with the group.

Boris   Bertie

BORIS AND BERTIE'S STORY

Aim of the story: To make clear the importance of taking turns.

1 Boris and Bertie are Charlie's cats.

2 They are playing in the garden.

3 Charlie calls them to come in for their dinner.

4 They run to go inside, but try to go through the cat flap at the same time.

5 They get stuck. Charlie has to help them.

6 Charlie explains why they must take turns.

| SESSION 5 |

Revision: Looking, Listening, Turn-Taking

1 The children put out the chairs.

2 Good sitting with music.

3 Play the 'Hello' game. At this stage, the game can be played in a different way without 'cueing in'. The child who is greeted returns the 'hello' with eye contact, then looks at and says 'hello' to someone else in the group, who continues in the same way. This goes on until everyone has had a turn. It is important to do this in a random way, so that every child keeps looking, in case he receives the greeting next.

4 *News Time.*

5 Homework task. Children show and share their toys.

6 Review and discuss the three stories about Molly, Florrie, and Boris and Bertie.

7 Play a listening and turn-taking game: 'My granny went to market and bought …'. The game involves each child repeating the phrase in turn, and adding an item such as carrots, candles, a pair of shoes, and so on, and remembering to say all the items already given. This activity is good for listening and recall.

8 *Snack Time.*

9 *Time-Line.*

10 Put away chairs and line up.

11 *Homework*: Everyone must bring in something – it could be a toy, a book, a photograph, or an object to show and talk about next week.

Talk About

SESSION 6

1 Children put out chairs.

2 Good sitting with music.

3 Play the 'Hello' game.

4 *News Time*.

5 Homework task. Children show and talk about the items they have brought in. Other children in the group should be encouraged to ask appropriate questions, so as to keep to topic. This is an opportunity to practise looking, listening and turn-taking.

6 Sing along to a tape. This will provide fun and light relief (for some), and is a good exercise for children with auditory sensitivity who find it difficult to tolerate music, certain sounds or frequencies, as well as loud noise.

7 *Snack Time*.

8 *Time-Line*.

9 Put away chairs and line up.

10 *Homework*: The children are asked to bring their favourite audio-tape to the next session.

SESSION 7

Being Friends
(and thinking about prepositions)

1. The children put out the chairs.

2. Good sitting with music.

3. Play the 'Hello' game.

4. *News Time.*

5. Homework task. The children show their tapes and talk about them. An adult decides how much time to spend on listening to them. After discussion, all the tapes are put into a bag and one is chosen to play.

6. Read the 'Oscar' story. Put across the idea that everyone finds some things difficult to do. What is a friend? (This may be very difficult for some children to grasp, and they may refer to sympathetic adults or even family members as friends.)

7. Play games to assess the understanding of prepositions (on, in, under, next to, by, in front of, behind, near). For example, put stickers on parts of the body or clothing; place objects in funny places, or ask the children to position themselves in relation to others.

8. *Snack Time.*

9. *Time-Line.*

10. Put away chairs and line up.

11. *Homework*: The children are asked to bring in a photo or draw a picture of a friend – that is, any child who is not related. Organise follow-up appointments with parents.

OSCAR'S STORY

Aim of the story: To help children understand what making friends is all about.

1 Oscar sometimes hurts other children and says unkind things to them.

2 The other children are upset, and do not want to play with him.

3 Oscar is sad and lonely and has no friends. Charlie wants to help him.

4 Charlie explains how other children feel when he is rough and unkind to them.

5 Charlie tells him what to do.

6 Oscar does as he is told and makes friends.

More About Friends

SESSION 8

1 The children put out the chairs.

2 Good sitting with music.

3 Play the 'Hello' game.

4 *News Time*.

5 Homework task. The children show the pictures of their friends and talk about them, giving information – for example, their name, their age, whether they are a boy or a girl.

6 Read the 'Charlie and Sally' story. Introduce the idea of pleasing others, as well as having personal likes and dislikes. Children contribute to a chart showing, for example, their favourite colour, favourite food or food disliked. Talk about filling in a family preferences chart for homework. They can choose their own topic – food, television programme, game, and so on.

7 *Snack Time*. Continue the theme of personal preferences and choices. Discuss how to refuse things without saying 'yuck'.

8 *Time-Line*. Talk about the ending of the group quite soon; who has enjoyed coming, and why.

9 Put away the chairs and line up.

10 *Homework*: Fill in a chart (see page 80) at home on family preferences.

SHEET FOR CHILDREN

SESSION 8 — Favourite Things Chart

	LIKES	DOES NOT LIKE
MUM		
DAD		
ME		
BROTHER		
SISTER		

Sally

CHARLIE AND SALLY

Aim of the story: Introduce the idea that everyone has different likes and dislikes, but they can still be friends.

1 Charlie and Sally are friends.

2 Charlie and Sally decide to have a picnic in the garden. Charlie says he will bring the food.

3 Charlie wants to bring chicken legs, crisps and biscuits.

4 Sally says she cannot eat chicken legs because she is a vegetarian, but she does eat crisps and biscuits.

5 Sally asks Charlie to bring salad and fruit for her to eat.

6 Charlie agrees and tells Sally that he likes fruit as well, but not salad.

How Am I Doing?

SESSION 9

1 The children put out the chairs.

2 Good sitting with music.

3 Play the 'Hello' game.

4 *News Time*.

5 Homework task. The children show their family charts and talk about them.

6 Read the 'Charlie is Asked Out' story. The children are encouraged to think about their own way of speaking – is it too loud or too soft; can people always understand them?

7 *Snack Time*. Discuss having a party next week for the last session. What would they like to eat and drink? What can they bring?

8 *Time-Line*.

9 Put away chairs and line up.

10 *Homework*: Ensure that parents are told, or that a note goes home about next week's party. They should discuss with their child what to bring, and then go shopping together to buy it.

Charlie

CHARLIE IS ASKED OUT

Aim of the story: To promote the idea of speaking in an appropriate way – not too loud and not too soft.

1 Charlie has a lot of friends who want to go out with him.

2 Doris asks him to go swimming, but she did not look at him and talked in a whisper. He did not hear her so did not go swimming.

3 Ollie using a shouting voice asked him to go out to a café, but Charlie did not want to go with him because the shouting gave him a headache.

4 Doris and Ollie feel sad.

5 Florrie asks Charlie to go to see a film, and Charlie says 'yes please'.

6 Florrie explains to Ollie and Doris how important it is to think about the way you are talking. Then next time they can all go out together.

SESSION 10

Having a Party – Saying Goodbye

1 The children put out the chairs.

2 Good sitting, with music.

3 Play the 'Hello' game.

4 *News Time*.

5 The children are reminded of all the things they have learnt in the group – looking, listening, taking turns, and so on. Remind them that these rules are for all times, and they should try to think about them, especially in school.

6 End of group party. The children are given a badge or certificate in recognition of their attendance and achievements (see page 161). It provides something to take away as an *aide-mémoire*.

7 *Time-Line*. Talk about the end of the group; relate it to events in the near future, such as Easter, Christmas, holidays, and so on.

8 Clear up and put away chairs, and say final goodbyes.

Remind parents to fill in their evaluation forms (Forms 5a and 5b, Appendix I), and to attend their individual follow-up meeting with the teacher and speech & language therapist. Stress that written reports on children's progress will follow.

Part III

7 to 11 year-olds

General Introduction

Generally, the information relating to younger age groups remains relevant – for example, the necessity to be flexible about the timing of the group sessions during term-time.

The criteria for admission will be broadly the same for this age group, and will accommodate children who are socially immature, as well as those who are socially impaired. These children can mix and gel as a group. Those likely to be problematic are children with overt EBD problems, who are liable to sabotage the success of the group by their behaviour. Indeed, any child whose behaviour is consistently challenging may have to be excluded if it is detrimental to the management of the group and the wellbeing of the other children.

If groups are organised within a special school, it should be possible to be more accommodating about children's individual needs. It is usually a matter for the speech & language therapist (SLT) and the child's teacher to assess their suitability for inclusion in a group.

It is still advisable to think in terms of the first two sessions as being a 'trial period', so that really unsuitable children can be excluded at an early stage. Parents will need to have this made clear to them at their initial workshop.

AIMS

Once again there is an assumption that the social skills introduced in the 3 to 5 years and 5 to 7 years programmes are now established and understood, at least in the structured setting of the group. However, it is not very likely that the skills will have been generalised. This means that children will need reminding about the basics of sitting, looking, listening and turn-taking. At this stage they may be very quick to comment on the shortcomings of others, but show remarkably little awareness of their own failings. Indeed, this 'reporting' on others can provide material for an entire session. Sorting out what constitutes 'nice things' to say is particularly relevant to the main theme at this level, which is relationships. Put simply, it is about getting on with other people.

At this level, the social skills stories and posters can be used as and when appropriate – for example, to recap when a target behaviour needs reinforcement; or to introduce a new topic, such as making friends.

Role play is introduced for this age group. It has proved to be a very useful technique, enabling children to assume appropriate behaviour in different situations. For example, learning how to refuse something with a modicum of good manners rather than saying 'yuck'.

PRACTICALITIES

Professionals involved in the running of social skills groups need to be on the lookout for new teaching aids and resources that can provide an additional dimension to group activities. For example, at the time of writing, two posters – 'Good Listening' and 'Good Talking' – have been published in the UK by Taskmaster. (A list of educational suppliers has been included in Appendix II.)

It is up to the professional to take what is useful and relevant from the earlier programmes. With this age group it should be possible to accommodate eight children. Pockets and badges will almost certainly continue to be useful. It is a good idea to make a chart that marks individual children's progress in using the basic skills. This encourages children to reflect on their own strengths and weaknesses, and thereby gain some insights into the mysteries of social interaction. The chart can be filled in at snack time and will make a good topic for group discussion. Parents can be shown the chart when they collect their children at the end of each session. Small representational logos can be drawn or stuck on the chart, by the teacher or speech & language therapist (SLT) or indeed the children:

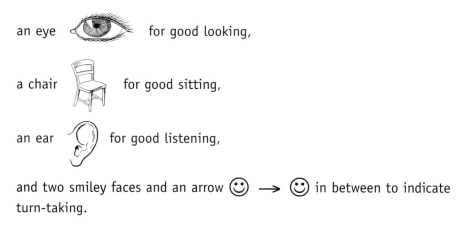

and two smiley faces and an arrow ☺ → ☺ in between to indicate turn-taking.

Samples of logos can be found on page 160.

The 'time-line' from the younger children's groups should now be replaced with a simple calendar to cover the 10 weeks of the group sessions. These should be individual and can be customised by each child. This forms a good initial homework task. A large calendar should be made and displayed to record things that apply to the group as a whole – for example, if a child knows he has to be absent for a hospital appointment, an exam or a school trip. Each week, a few moments should be spent checking the group calendar poster.

For the final session, design certificates of achievement. Each child should be asked to record what he has learnt to do in the group, and what is still difficult (homework session 9). This information can be included in the certificate, a sample design for which can be found on page 161.

> **SESSION 1**

Meetings & Greetings

1 The children put out the chairs.

2 Start with good sitting, to music.

3 *Greetings*. This indicates moving on from the 'Hello' game as played at the infant level. At this stage, children should be helped to use greetings in a more spontaneous way. They can benefit from specific requests to look at and greet the group leader when they come into the room. They should be encouraged to think of different greetings, such as 'Hello', 'Good morning/afternoon', and even 'Hi'. The routine of saying goodbye at the end of the session can also be addressed, again with attention to variations such as 'See you next week', 'Have a good weekend/holiday', 'See you soon' and 'Goodbye and thank you'.

This exercise marks an introduction to role play. It is always necessary for the adult to model what is required, so that individuals in the group know what is expected of them. Sometimes it is helpful to suggest that role play is like acting, and most children will know what this is about from nativity plays, assemblies and end-of-term shows.

A good way to check on the children's spontaneous use of greetings is to note how they respond to any visitors to the group. They may need help over appropriate ways to introduce themselves.

4 Why are we here? From this point on, children need to have a clear understanding about why they are coming to the group. Introduce the idea that everyone in the group needs some help with such things as talking to people, knowing how to behave and how to get on with others, especially other children. Do other children pick on them? Each child can be asked in turn what they think applies to them.

5 *Group Rules*. Explain that in order for everyone to enjoy coming to the group, there have to be some rules. The children should be encouraged to think of these for themselves. They may include not interrupting, not being late, not being rude or unkind, and giving others a chance to have their say. Everyone helps to write the rules on a poster.

6 *News Time*. At this level children can be advised that they can give different kinds of news. Personal news will be about things they or their families have done or are going to do. School news will be about things going on in school – trips,

MEETINGS & GREETINGS

problems, work topics, and changes of staff perhaps. World news will be about things seen on television or heard about through the media. Discussion of world events and even disasters often reveals time and again that knowing about something is not the same as really understanding it. Knowledge is likely to be very fragmented.

SESSION 1

7 *Snack Time*.

8 *Calendar*. Fill in the group calendar poster.

9 Ask the children to put away the chairs and line up. Don't forget to remind them to say their goodbyes.

10 *Homework*: Give out individual calendars and ask the children to fill them in, showing things they want to record such as family birthdays, weekly clubs and activities. Parents can be informed about homework tasks via a home/school notebook, or printed sheets concerning all sessions (Appendix I, Form 4b).

| SESSION 2 | # Manners

1 The children put out the chairs.

2 Commence with good sitting to music. At this stage it may be appropriate to talk about how the music makes us feel. Why do we listen to the music? Why do we have it at the start of the group? Suggest to the children that listening to music is a good way to put aside things that have upset them and might prevent them from being good group members. In future weeks, before the music, each child will have a chance to say if they are feeling upset about something. The music provides a marker to enable children to set aside what has gone on earlier in the day, such as family disputes, a stressful journey, even excitement in the classroom. They are then more likely to be receptive in the group session. (Children with autism commonly find it difficult to shake off a negative mood or state of mind, which then pervades everything they subsequently encounter.)

3 Discuss whether everyone in the group remembered to give a greeting when they arrived. Give praise or reminders, as appropriate.

4 *News Time*. At this stage, introduce rules for giving news. Everyone has to take a turn, with no opting out. There must be no interruptions, but the children can ask the news-giver appropriate questions to get more information. The speaker should be encouraged to state what sort of news they are going to give – whether it is personal family news, school news or world news.

5 *Homework review*: Look at everyone's calendar and make comparisons and connections.

6 Introduce the concept of **manners.** Make the point that if you are by yourself it doesn't matter how you behave. Manners are about how we get along with other people. Talk about what constitutes bad manners, including burping, farting, grabbing, picking your nose, eating with your mouth open, and so on. This is an opportunity to pinpoint any examples of bad manners in the group. Put the question 'Will people like you if you …?'

7 *Snack Time*. Think about good manners while eating and drinking.

8 *Calendar*.

9 The children put away the chairs, line up and say their goodbyes.

10 *Homework*: Ask the parents to encourage their child to think of a situation when they would need to practise good manners. They must be able to talk about it at the next session.

More About Manners

SESSION 3

1 The children put out the chairs.

2 Encourage good sitting to music, as before.

3 Discuss whether everyone in the group remembered to give a greeting when they arrived. Give praise or reminders, as appropriate.

4 *News Time*.

5 *Homework review*: Children talk about their examples of good manners.

6 Expand on the concept of manners. Role play to show good and bad manners. Suggested topics are: Saying sorry; Saying thank you, even when it is something which is not wanted; How to say no*; Holding the door open; Not pushing in; Not butting in; and Thinking about how to be helpful.

7 *Snack Time*. Check for good manners – is there any need for prompts? Encourage and praise offers to help clear away – this is practise at being helpful. Continue to monitor in future sessions.

8 *Calendar*.

9 The children put away the chairs, line up and say their goodbyes.

10 *Homework*: Ask the parents to help their child list six words or phrases that indicate good manners. For example: please, thank you, may I, excuse me, and sorry.

*In some situations or circumstances, it might be appropriate to talk about saying no in the context of personal safety.

| SESSION 4 | # Friends |

1 The children put out the chairs.

2 Practise good sitting to music, as before.

3 Greetings – give praise or reminders, as appropriate.

4 *News Time*.

5 *Homework review*: Children compare their lists of good manners words. Expand into what it means to be polite.

6 Recap 'Will people like you if …?' (Session 2), and discuss aspects of interpersonal behaviour such as being kind, helping, wanting to win, sharing, butting in, hurting, saying nasty things, calling names, teasing and bullying (group leaders can use this session to introduce any issues relevant to the group). Which sort of behaviour will make people like you?

7 This is an appropriate context in which to introduce the notion of *flexibility*. Children with social communication problems inevitably have great difficulties in being flexible in most aspects of daily life. It is helpful to spend time giving them a clear and tangible means of understanding the concept of flexibility. A comparison between a rigid approach to tasks and a more flexible one can be demonstrated, using a piece of card as a visual aid, to illustrate the difference between rigidity and flexibility. Children need to understand that they have to be able to bend, like the piece of card, to deal with changes and demands that will inevitably occur. Changes may be the cause of great anxiety to some, or result in inappropriate behaviour in others. This topic should be further explored by discussing instances of change and appropriate strategies that could be put into practice. It is not necessary to go into too much detail in this session. However, once the topic has been approached, it should be reinforced in later sessions whenever it is appropriate.

8 Begin to discuss friends. What does this mean?*

9 *Snack Time*.

10 *Calendar*.

11 The children put away the chairs, line up and say their goodbyes.

12 *Homework*: Ask parents to help their child look for pictures in papers or magazines showing people doing things together – that is, being friends.

*The concept of friendship is complex, and needs to be approached at a slow pace, and with flexibility. It is always useful to use whatever is generated by the group – their ideas about friendship may be idiosyncratic or skewed. It may be possible to link up with mainstream school initiatives such as 'circle time', 'circle of friends', or 'buddy schemes'.

SESSION 4

SESSION 5 — More About Friends

1 The children put out the chairs.

2 Extend the time for good sitting with music by a minute or two.

3 Give reminders about greetings, if this is still necessary.

4 *News Time.*

5 Introduce the 'Charlie and Sally' story (page 82). This will help the group to think about what it means to have a friend, taking turns, sharing, and doing what the other person wants to do.

6 Link the story to last week's homework. Talk about what people are doing together in the pictures. Perhaps make a collage. Everyone has a chance to say the name of their friend. It is important that children are guided away from naming inappropriate people as friends, such as relations, teachers, or even their bus driver.

7 *Snack Time.*

8 *Calendar.*

9 The children put away the chairs, line up and say their goodbyes.

10 *Homework*: The children are asked to bring a photograph or make a drawing of a friend, and to be ready to talk about what they like doing together.

Feelings

SESSION 6

1 The children put out the chairs.

2 Expect a few minutes of good sitting, with music.

3 *News Time.*

4 *Homework review.* The children take turns to show their photographs or drawings of their friend; to say their name, and what they like doing together. (The group leader must be prepared to deal with the child who has no friends but would like them, and others who prefer their own company.)

5 Move on to a discussion about how everyone is different. Play the game 'What I like best' to highlight individual tastes and differences. This is where the children are asked to name such things as their favourite food, television programme, game, and so on.

6 *Snack Time.*

7 *Calendar.* Highlight any social activities with friends this week.

8 The children put away the chairs, line up, and say their goodbyes.

9 *Homework*: The children are to ask their parents and other family members about their favourite things, and be able to talk about them next week.

SESSION 7 — More About Feelings

1 The children put out the chairs.

2 Expect a few minutes of good sitting, with music.

3 *News Time*.

4 *Homework review*. The children take turns to talk about their family members' favourite things. Inevitably, some children may want to talk incessantly. The use of a timer or stop-watch can be useful to move things on and reinforce the notion of turn-taking.

5 Play the body-language game 'Guess how I'm feeling'. The adults model a range of body postures and gestures to indicate feelings such as boredom, tiredness, sadness, excitement, anger, fear, interest, attention, and shyness.

6 Play a game of 'How would you feel if ...?' A selection of cards identifying a range of situations are offered, and the children take turns to talk about how they would respond. Suggestions include losing a pet; going to a football match; having to stay in at playtime; breaking their mum's best vase; seeing a scary television programme or film; having a long wait at a supermarket checkout; taking part in class assembly at school; being teased at school, or someone accidentally breaking their favourite toy.

7 *Snack Time*. The children are asked to use gesture instead of speech.

8 *Calendar*.

9 The children put away the chairs.

10 *Homework*: Children are asked to cut out pictures of people from papers and magazines that show different feelings.

Meaning

SESSION 8

1 The children put out the chairs.

2 Allow time for good sitting with music, as usual. Follow this with talking about how everyone is feeling today.

3 *News Time*.

4 *Homework review*. The children show their newspaper pictures; talk about them, and discuss what the people might be saying or thinking. The adults will need to provide some pictures in case the children's contributions are inappropriate! A collage poster can be made with the contributions. Speech or thought bubbles can be added. Do people always mean what they say? Introduce the idea of hidden meaning. This can be done by saying to the children, for example, 'Suppose your room was really messy and untidy, and mum said, "What a lovely tidy room!!", would she mean it?' Or else if she said 'Your room is a pigsty!', would that be true?

5 *Snack Time*.

6 *Calendar*.

7 The children put away the chairs.

8 *Homework*: Hand out a worksheet asking the children to find out what the following idioms mean:

>   It's raining cats and dogs.
>   You've hit the nail on the head.
>   To pull your socks up.
>   To have a frog in your throat.
>   To let the cat out of the bag.
>   To get in a stew.

Can the children produce an extra one of their own? They are advised to ask parents or their teacher for help.

NB. Ask parents for a small financial contribution for a special snack time during the last group session.

SESSION 8 — What do these idioms mean?

If you don't know, ask somebody.

Write your answers in the spaces. You can draw pictures too if you like.

1 It's raining cats and dogs.

2 You've hit the nail on the head.

3 To pull your socks up.

4 To have a frog in your throat.

5 To let the cat out of the bag.

6 To get in a stew.

Can you think of one other idiom? If you can, write it down and explain what it means.

More About Meaning

SESSION 9

1 The children put out the chairs.

2 Good sitting, with music.

3 *News Time.*

4 *Homework review.* The children are asked to read from their worksheets in turn to explain the meaning of the idioms that they were given last week. Has there been any success in finding new ones?

5 *Snack Time.*

6 *Calendar.* Highlight the fact that next week is the last session.

7 Talk about a special snack time next week. The children can suggest things that they would like to eat.

8 *Homework*: The children are asked to think about what has happened in the group. A worksheet is provided for them to fill in.

  a What did they like best about the group?

  b What have they learnt?

  c What is still difficult?

WORKSHEET

SESSION 9

Name

Date

What have you liked best about the group?

What do you feel you have learnt?

What do you still find difficult?

Reflecting

SESSION 10

1 The children put out the chairs.

2 A final opportunity for the children to demonstrate good sitting, with music.

3 *News Time*.

4 *Homework review*. Discuss the children's worksheets. How do they feel about the end of the group? What will happen next? Would they like to come to another group?

5 *Snack Time* with 'frills' (as planned in Session 9).

6 Keeping in touch. How can we do this? Facilitate the distribution of addresses, telephone numbers and e-mail addresses (subject to parental agreement). It is important that the professional does not undertake this. The children themselves should be involved in thinking about how this can be done, and they and their parents should be encouraged to make the arrangements for themselves. Since many children with social difficulties want friends, contacts made in the group should be nurtured. 'Keeping in touch' is a very positive and valuable adjunct to the ending of the group.

The majority of friendships that develop are likely to be based on a shared, possibly eccentric interest, rather than interpersonal attributes. Nevertheless, such relationships should be encouraged by every means possible, as they have the potential to enhance the quality of the children's lives. Such spin-offs as visiting each other; using the telephone; planning and making arrangements, and developing conversational skills are valuable social experiences.

7 Award 'achievement' certificates (see page 161).

8 Ask the children to put away the chairs and to say their farewells.

Follow-on Sessions
(7 to 11 year-olds)

Because circumstances can be so variable, and because we advocate flexibility, it may be helpful to include additional topics that can be used to replace particular session plans; to extend the group beyond 10 weeks; or to link in with the national curriculum in the UK. The topics may also be of use to deal with specific or current issues that emerge as the children mature and enter adolescence; indeed, some of the topics included in the list at the end of the programme for older children may well be relevant.

- Caring for pets.

- What is a vegetarian?

- Eating out – where to go, what to choose, and how to behave.

- Going on holiday.

- Changes in school – from one class to another, to a new school.

- Moving house.

- Families.

- Using books. The series of 'feelings' books by Moses and Gordon (1993 and 1997) listed in Appendix II can provide material for at least a term's sessions. Publishing for children including those with special needs has burgeoned, and new titles appear all the time. Those running groups only have to keep their eyes open for inspiration.

- Current events in the news – even disasters, if they impinge on group members. For example, earthquakes or floods may impact on children with relations in areas affected.

SOCIAL STORIES

'Social Stories' have been used as a specific approach by Carol Gray (see Appendix II), to enable children with autism to cope with social situations as they occur. It involves the adult writing simple stories to clarify potentially confusing scenarios. The aim is to make it easier for the children to understand what is going on; what is expected of them, and how to join in and enjoy different experiences. Although the approach is designed for the child as an individual, there is no reason why the method cannot be used for a group, and for children other than those who have autism.

The stories should have a ratio of 2:5 descriptive and/or perspective sentences, and 0:1 directive and/or control sentences. The story should always be well within a child's comprehension level, with appropriate vocabulary and print size. An example adapted from *The New Social Story Book* (see Appendix II) is given below.

Playing Video Games

Sometimes I play video games.

I have lots of games to choose from. Not everyone has as many video games as me.

I might play by myself, or I might play with someone else.

We take turns playing video games.

Sometimes I win a game, and sometimes I lose.

It is OK if I lose. I will try to be a good sport. A good sport is someone who plays fair.

A good sport does not get angry if he loses.

NB. The only directive sentence is 'I will try to be a good sport'. The rest is either descriptive or perspective.

Social Skills Programmes

Part IV

Older Children & Adolescents 11 to 16 year-olds

General Information

When setting up a social skills group for older children, professionals need to ascertain whether the skills that were introduced in the earlier programmes for younger children have really been established. If there are doubts about this, it is most important that a short introductory course is offered prior to the official start of the group. Since, as stated earlier, the candidates for the group are required to have normal cognitive abilities, it should be possible to introduce the basic prerequisites of good sitting, looking, listening, turn-taking and not interrupting, within two 'lead-in' sessions. This does not imply that the participants will be able to put these skills into practice in the two sessions. The intention is that they will become familiar with the concepts and language to be used in the group. It may be practical to consider these prerequisites as a component of group rules, and helpful to have them written down, both as handouts and as a poster. Although the 'lead-in' group may require frequent reminders about the rules, more advanced participants may have lapses, and the reminders will not come amiss for them.

For this age group the content of the social skills sessions should link up with relevant topics within the school curriculum. It may tie in with religious education, personal and social education, life skills or general studies. What is important is that it relates directly to the lives of the participants, both in school and in the wider community. Working with this age group can be rewarding and great fun, as at this stage much can come from the young people themselves to form the basis for a stimulating and reciprocal learning experience. It is difficult to be prescriptive about the optimum number of group participants as there are so many variables to consider, not least the range and severity of communication difficulties. It may be viable to go up to 10 or 12 in some cases.

Although we have kept to the 10-session format for this age group, we have included some ideas for 'add-on' sessions as a social skills element may be ongoing in the curricular areas referred to above. Indeed, we would recommend that every effort is made to ensure that this is so. It is not difficult to plan a social skills curriculum to extend over a whole academic year and this would, of course, give greater scope for more detailed work on specific aspects of social communication. For example, in term one the focus could be on **feelings**. This could cover such things as the language used to express feelings; identifying the feelings in self and others, and feelings expressed through body language, etc. The subject matter for term two could be considered under the heading of **what words mean**. This would include work on aspects of language that are confusing, such as inference, metaphor and idiom. The programme for term three should ideally be practical; **out and about** is a useful heading to focus the group's attention on the social language needed for dealing with situations in the wider community beyond school – for example, shopping, making telephone calls, leaving messages, asking for advice, or making complaints. If the sessions include outings, there will be financial implications, as well as obtaining parental consent. The complications engendered by such considerations may deter group leaders from attempting the activities. However, even if this is the case, much can be done with role play and a few props.

Regardless of how the social skills groups are organised, flexibility is absolutely vital, and those running the group should be sensitive and responsive to issues and events as they arise. This will allow matters such as bullying, bereavement, divorce, births, weddings, current events and global concerns to be introduced into the sessions and discussed or dealt with as appropriate. It may be necessary to extend news time to accommodate unscheduled topics. Alternatively, these topics can be introduced as follow-on session topics (see page 136).

QUESTIONS OF DIAGNOSIS

Some children attending the group will almost undoubtedly have a diagnosis of an autistic spectrum disorder or Asperger Syndrome. In the past, it was accepted practice not to discuss diagnostic issues with such individuals. We now know through personal contact, as well as articles and books written by able people with autism, that this is not at all helpful. All are adamant that knowing what was the matter had a very positive effect on their quality of life. It enabled them to understand why aspects of their lives were so difficult, and was the key to making appropriate life choices. In addition, the diagnosis assisted them in gaining access to understanding and support. We would therefore encourage discussion on diagnostic issues at the outset. Some young people will already be aware of their diagnosis, while others may be in complete ignorance, possibly because a diagnosis has never been made.

Diagnosis is a very sensitive issue and can be discussed fully at the Parent Workshop to ascertain attitudes and feelings. If parents are in agreement, the subject could be approached in the first session, 'Why Are We Here?', by discussing what members of the group find difficult. This should focus on an array of social difficulties, both overt and subtle, and it may then be appropriate to move on to the question of diagnosis and diagnostic labels. Young people whose difficulties are not considered to be autistic in nature will also benefit from attending a social skills group. Some may have a specific learning difficulty, or speech and language problems; others may exhibit social naivety and immaturity. Social skills groups are also beneficial for young people who are immoderately shy and lacking in self-confidence. Indeed, such a group provides the ultimate setting for social inclusion, with opportunities for practising all aspects of communication free of peer pressure, teasing and criticism.

SNACK TIME

It is certainly worth retaining this slot. It still provides an incentive, and at this stage it is very important that young people know what is, or is not, appropriate to take from a plate on offer – and indeed how to offer! They should be encouraged to organise this activity for themselves, including the kind of drinks they want to have. Tea, coffee and hot chocolate may be a good idea, with responsibilities assigned to organising boiling water, offering milk and sugar, and so on. Shopping for the refreshments is an additional activity and can involve many life skills, including thinking about value for money, choices, likes and dislikes, and locating items on supermarket shelves. Snack time can provide an opportunity for the group to interact with each other in a more natural and informal way.

SOCIAL PITFALLS

It is always necessary to tackle social gaffes as and when they occur, or even when reported by other adults in contact with the young people. For example, going into the school library and not recognising that a pile of books and a coat over a chair denotes that that place is already occupied; remembering, for example, that other people may expect to be asked how they are. More often than not, those with social difficulties assume that if nothing is said by the person, it is not necessary to ask. They may need reminding that if they do not have the answer to a question, they should not ignore it, but still need to respond in some way. Group members can be encouraged to think of suitable responses for themselves, such as 'I don't know', 'I'm not sure', or 'I don't understand'. At this stage there is going to be a focus on body language, and in conjunction with this, the young people need to consider aspects of their own behaviour and its possible effect on others. For example, a young man with a liking for the front seat in the bus stood close behind the occupant – an elderly lady who felt thoroughly intimidated. He simply wanted her to go and sit somewhere else so that he could take over her seat, and had no idea that his behaviour could be seen as threatening.

It may seem devious, but outsider information about any inappropriate behaviour of group members can be used constructively in group sessions as a focus for special attention. There is no necessity to personalise the information, since dealing with the problems in general terms is effective and less liable to cause upset, or even resentment. When the topic of boasting was discussed in a group of teenagers, the perpetrator commented to one of the adults after the session 'I think I do that'.

ROLE PLAY

This technique, which was introduced at 7–11 year-old level, should be developed and incorporated into the sessions wherever possible. For example, the situation above concerning the young man on the bus could be used very easily for role play. Group members could practise acting out different ways of looking at the situation from the perspectives of both the elderly lady and the young man. Modelling by the adults will continue to be a necessary component of role play.

Group Rules & Why Are We Here?

SESSION 1

1 Welcome and greetings.

2 *Setting out group rules.* While group members should be encouraged to contribute their own ideas, some baseline rules should be presented at the outset. The cognitive level of group members will determine the sort of language that can be used. The following suggestions may be helpful, but be careful not to overload the group with too many:

- Remember to sit still on your chair without rocking, fidgeting or lolling.
- When talking to someone it is important to look at them.
- Listen to what other people have to say.
- Remember not to talk for too long, so that everyone has a turn.
- Everyone in the group is equal.
- There must be no rudeness or name-calling.
- Everyone has a right to be heard without interruption.
- There must be no opting out.

3 *Why are we here?* (Use a flipchart to list ideas that can be referred to in later sessions.) To start on a positive note, give everyone an opportunity to say what they think they are good at. The group then moves on to consider things that they find difficult. Almost certainly the adults will have to give a lead, since the initial aim is to focus on personal, social and interactive difficulties, rather than a lack of capability in drawing, maths or reading, for example.

The sort of difficulties that are likely to emerge might include:

- Understanding what people mean.
- Understanding jokes.
- Knowing what to do about being bullied.
- Coping with crowds of people.
- Making friends.
- Knowing how to ask for help or information.
- Getting organised.
- Feeling anxious or worried about many things.

The group needs to be told that these are the topics that will be worked on in the coming weeks.

SESSION 1

(If appropriate, these difficulties can be linked with possible diagnoses. These are likely to include Autism, Autistic Spectrum Disorder, Asperger Syndrome, ADHD, Dyslexia and Dyspraxia.)

4 *News Time*. Introduce the topic and discuss what is expected of everybody. Explain that, starting next week, all group members will be expected to give some news. The news could be personal, to do with school, or relate to current affairs.

5 *Snack Time*. Explain the options and what is required of everybody in the group.

6 *Focus for the week*. Remind the group about regular attendance. What should happen if they cannot attend for any reason? How will they remember to come every week?

7 Tidy the room and say goodbyes.

How Do We Feel?

SESSION 2

1 Ensure that all group members have given an appropriate greeting.

2 Listen to music.

3 *News Time*.

4 *Introduce the topic of feelings*. It is not unusual to discover that many young people with social difficulties have a very limited vocabulary for describing and talking about feelings. Happy and sad may be the sum total for dealing with the gamut of human emotions. It is therefore necessary to enhance their awareness and understanding of more subtle feelings, such as disappointment, anxiety or embarrassment. This can be done in a variety of ways, depending on the availability of commercially produced resources. For example, a poster showing a range of appropriately labelled facial expressions is good, but if one is not available, it should be possible to create one using magazine pictures and photographs. Group members can be encouraged to link their feelings to those on display. They can then be asked, for example, 'What would make you feel disappointed?' One boy, when asked this question, insisted that he never felt disappointed. The SLT running the group then had to remind him of how he felt when a school trip that he was really excited about was cancelled because of the weather.

5 *Snack Time*.

6 *Focus for the Week*. Everybody in the group needs to spend time during the week thinking about their feelings in relation to things that happen. Remind them that this will be talked about next week.

7 Tidy the room and say goodbyes.

| SESSION 3 |

Body Language

1 Ensure that greetings have been made, as before.

2 Listen to music.

3 *News Time.*

4 Refer to last week's session, and ask for a few volunteers to talk about things that happened to them during the past week, and how they felt. It is more than likely that the adults will have to take the lead so that participants know what is required of them. Steer away from happy/sad responses, and encourage them to think about and use such terms as worried, disappointed, bored and excited.

5 Present the idea that you can sometimes guess how people are feeling by looking at their **body language**. Start off with a game whereby adults adopt a range of postures that depict particular feelings. The group members are asked to identify what feelings are being presented and, once they have understood, they can then take turns themselves. The game can be extended – for example, a sheet can be used so that only hands or feet are visible to convey emotion or, alternatively, people can show feelings in the way they walk or move. These games should be conducted in a light-hearted way so that participants are happy to have a go and try things out for themselves. This will lead naturally on to role play in later sessions. Not all group members will necessarily have had experience of this, and as teenagers they are likely to be reluctant to 'perform'.

6 *Snack Time.*

7 *Focus for the Week.* Everybody in the group needs to think about body language during the coming week, noting it in other people and thinking about what messages they may be giving to others in the way they sit, stand and move.

8 Tidy the room and say goodbyes.

Conversation Skills

SESSION 4

1 Ensure that all group members have given an appropriate greeting.

2 Listen to music.

3 *News Time*.

4 Review body language. Ask for a few volunteers to give examples of their observations of body language. The aim is to use any examples for discussion. Explain to the group that from now on we need to check on our own and each other's body language, to ensure that we are giving the right impression. For example, anyone sprawling or rocking on their chair will be identified and asked to reflect on how this appears to others. If parents agree, it may be helpful to make use of a Polaroid camera or a video camera to highlight body language.

5 Introduce the topic of **conversation**. What do group members understand by this? Discuss the difference between talking *at* people and talking *with* people. Identify the key elements of conversation:

- Looking at the person you are talking to.
- Listening to what the other person is saying.
- Not interrupting.
- Taking turns.
- Keeping to the same topic.
- Not fidgeting.
- Respecting other people's space.
- Not talking too loudly, or too softly.
- Not making personal remarks.
- Not talking for too long.

All these elements need elaboration and explanation. All future sessions should include reference to this important, if not central, aspect of communication.

6 *Snack Time*. Suggest to the group that snack time provides a very good opportunity for practising conversation skills. Remind them of similar situations at school or in college – at break times and lunch times when they meet up with their peers in the canteen.

7 *Focus for the Week*. Ask all group members to recall any opportunity they have in the coming week to think about or practise conversational skills.

8 Tidy the room and say goodbyes.

| SESSION 5 | # Issues & Problems

1 Greetings, as before. It is advisable not to give reminders about greetings every week, as it is important to assess spontaneity.

2 Listen to music.

3 *News Time.*

4 All group members are asked to report on opportunities they have had in the week to practise conversational skills.

5 Introduce the topic of problems that group members experience in their daily lives. Refer back to the list that was compiled in Session 1 (page 123, item 3) and add additional specific issues – for example, teasing; knowing what to say, and even how to recognise dangerous situations that they may be led into by others. Whatever topics emerge, they should be explored in some detail. The young person who complains about being bullied or teased may in fact be a perpetrator in certain situations. Always follow up assertions with the question 'Do you ever do that to others?', if there is some evidence from a teacher or another child of this happening. However, be aware of the advice in the introduction to this age group about not personalising issues too forcibly.

In an ideal world, or in educational settings where the groups are class-based and ongoing, there are likely to be daily opportunities to explore these issues in many different situations. Since this may not be an option for the majority of young people, it is important to involve a named teacher or support assistant to follow up issues that emerge for a particular group member. If at all possible, that member of staff should attend as many group sessions as possible, to enable them to support that group member more effectively in school.

The choice of issues to be tackled, and the ways in which the problems are approached, must be at the discretion of the professionals running the group. The choice may be determined because of an untoward episode affecting a particular young person. Whatever issues are to be tackled, sensitivity is essential.

6 *Snack Time.*

7 *Focus for the Week.* All group members need to identify a problem or difficulty that they will try to tackle and talk about next week. The aim is for everyone to consider useful strategies, and perhaps gain some insights.

8 Tidy the room and say goodbyes.

What Words Mean

SESSION 6

1 Expect greetings, as before.

2 Listen to music.

3 *News Time*.

4 Refer to last week's session, and ask for volunteers to talk about any problems that they had to deal with during the past week. It is important to ensure that it is not always the same individuals who volunteer. However, in some groups, the more timid may actually benefit when others take the initiative. It provides them with a model on which to base their own contributions. Sometimes, of course, it is necessary for the adults running the group to take the lead.

5 Introduce the topic of 'what words mean'. The easiest way to embark on this topic is to present some common idioms and establish whether the group finds them meaningful, or takes them literally. Some group members may have been introduced to this topic in a social skills group at the 7 to 11 year level. The most commonly used idioms, such as 'raining cats and dogs'; 'let the cat out of the bag', and 'getting too big for his boots' are useful at the outset to introduce or revise the topic. However, the aim is to move on to more subtle and sophisticated examples, such as:

> Cloud cuckoo land.
>
> Taken for a ride.
>
> Back to square one.
>
> Room to swing a cat.
>
> Turn the tables on.
>
> Get the upper hand.
>
> A white elephant.
>
> Get blood out of a stone.
>
> Blows hot and cold.

There is no reason for selecting these particular idioms, any will do. The purpose of this exercise is to develop understanding and appreciation that words may carry ambiguous messages. In general, it may not be helpful to encourage group members to use these idioms for themselves at this stage, since they are likely to

SESSION 6

do this in a mechanical and rigid way. At a later stage, however, they may be able to incorporate idiomatic language with spontaneity.

6 *Snack Time.*

7 *Focus for the Week.* Group members are asked to complete a worksheet listing some less common idioms.

8 Tidy the room and say goodbyes.

WORKSHEET

What Words Mean

SESSION 6

Write down the meanings of these idioms. If you get stuck, you may have to ask someone for help.

1 Cuckoo in the nest.

2 Keep a low profile.

3 Down to earth.

4 Butterfingers.

5 Have a bee in one's bonnet.

6 Spill the beans.

| SESSION 7 | # More About What Words Mean |

1 Greetings.*

2 Listen to music.

3 *It may be appropriate to spend some time discussing the subject of meetings and greetings. At this stage, young people are likely to come into contact with more people, reflecting the fact that they are growing up and that the world is changing for them as they move beyond childhood. They should be encouraged to consider how they can adapt their language style in different situations and with different people. This can be approached in the following way (role play will be particularly helpful here):

How do you greet your friends/mates? Everyone tries to think of an example; check for appropriacy, but remember that greetings, like idioms, are subject to fads and fashions. How do you greet adults you know well, such as teachers or family friends? How would you greet adults you do not know well, especially at a first meeting? Also consider ways of signing off and saying goodbye. Remind group members of the concept of flexibility (see 7 to 11 Years Programme, Session 4).

4 *News Time.*

5 Refer to last week's worksheet on idioms, and move on to talk about ambiguity. Words and phrases can have many different meanings that may depend on how they are said and the tone of voice used. What are sarcasm and irony? Do the group recognise lies (including the white variety)? Group leaders need to have a supply of examples illustrating these aspects of language, such as 'What a lovely tidy room!' when it is a mess, 'I love washing up your dirty mugs', or 'Thank you for the lovely present' (on being given yet another boring pair of socks).

6 *Snack Time.*

7 *Focus for the Week.* All group members are asked to recall giving a specific greeting during the week. Those who watch soaps on television can make a note of the ways in which the characters greet each other.

8 Tidy the room and say goodbyes (are they appropriate?).

Having & Giving

SESSION 8

1 Greetings. Link this to last week's focus, and ask for comments about greetings in television soaps.

2 Listen to music.

3 *News Time*.

4 Introduce the topic of 'having and giving'. Catalogues are very useful for this topic, particularly those that include a wide range of everyday articles (in the UK, the Argos catalogue, for example, is particularly useful). The pages can be removed and the pictures cut out as necessary for the topic. Work can focus on a range of options, and the following list gives a few ideas for some activities:

- Choosing clothes for themselves, for specific occasions such as discos, holidays and school.
- Choosing suitable presents for different age groups, from toddlers to grandparents, friends and even other group members.
- Choosing things for the home or for their room, both items that are useful and those that are decorative.

The aim of this exercise is to encourage group members to consider the interests, needs and circumstances of others. For example, group members could be asked to select a present for mum for Mothers' Day. The pile of cut-out pictures should include items of interest to group members as well as items that might be suitable for the recipient, though not necessarily gender specific. Group members have to give reasons for their choices. If unsuitable choices are made, they should be helped to reflect on the criteria for making better ones. Have they taken into account the age of the person; the person's home situation, their interests and what they may already have? The cost of items is, of course, important, and it is advisable to suggest a price limit at the outset to avoid excursions into the world of fantasy.

5 *Snack Time*.

6 *Focus for the Week*. Provide group members with a list of high street shops and a map of the area – for example, in the UK, Woolworths, Marks & Spencer, WH Smith, Boots, Gap, Bodyshop and Mothercare. They should mark the location of each shop on their map, and record the sort of articles that would be on sale in each one.

7 Tidy the room and say goodbyes.

> **SESSION 9**

Out and About, and Shopping

1 Greetings.

2 Listen to music.

3 *News Time.*

4 The aim of this session is to be as close to real-life experiences as possible, which ideally should involve going out and about in the locality.

Discuss going shopping linked to last week's focus on specific High Street shops. Group members could be asked for directions to locate specific shops, as well as public telephones, the police station, the post office, and where to go for a snack.

It may be appropriate to suggest specific shopping objectives. For example, group members could be asked to find toilet items they would need for going on a week's holiday.

Going out for a meal such as a pizza or burger, taking into account vegetarians and other specific dietary preferences, is a good and popular exercise. Even if it is not possible to organise such an expedition for practical reasons, role play can provide opportunities for learning how to deal with such things as ordering and deciding where to sit, as well as paying.

Bearing in mind individual preferences, the group can plan a party to mark the final group session. Is it viable for each group member to invite one guest? The guest should be a parent, teacher or learning support assistant rather than a peer, since the event is in effect an episode of intervention and will facilitate appraisal of individual group members' progress. Any observations can be discussed with parents and/or professionals at the interview following the end of the group. The final session will be split between shopping for the party and the party itself. Decisions will need to be made about food, drink and music choices.

5 *Snack Time.*

6 Tidy the room and say goodbyes.

Party Time

SESSION 10

It may be necessary to extend this session, as it includes a party.

1 Greetings.

2 Discuss the timetable for shopping and party preparations.
Prepare a shopping list, based on last week's preferences and availability.
Allocate responsibilities – who buys what; who prepares food and drink.
Plan for visitors and how will they be greeted.
Remind group members about their social behaviour when offering food and drink to guests.
Check that the person in charge of music has the necessary discs and tapes.

3 As the party is an unstructured situation, it is a good opportunity to put into practice the skills that have been introduced in earlier sessions. Group members need to be reminded of this before any guests arrive.

4 *The Party*

5 The party can be followed by a brief evaluation of the event with the group, and clearing up.

Do any group members wish to keep in touch? If so, addresses and telephone numbers should be exchanged.

With this age group, a follow-up social evening two or three months hence may be appropriate to ascertain progress. It will also provide an opportunity for group members to discuss whether they need further support.

Suggestions for follow-on sessions are listed on pages 136–7.

Follow-on Sessions
(Older Children & Adolescents)

- Soaps and other television programmes discussing relationships and behaviour. For example, do they approve or disapprove of the ways certain characters behave? Can they describe the characters?

- Art appreciation. Group members are given a copy of a print, and are asked to provide information about it. For example, does it depict times past or the present day? If it is a portrait, how is the subject feeling? Do they like or dislike the picture, and what are their reasons? Would they like to hang it on a wall at home?

- Uses for strange objects such as ornaments, bric-à-brac, kitchen gadgets and utensils. This is an opportunity for some lateral thinking. Many people have access to an object or item the function of which is not immediately clear. Group members can have a lot of fun guessing its possible use and suggesting their own ideas.

- Using the telephone. This should include public telephones, using both money and cards. Group members can practise asking for information, or leaving a message on an answer machine. Since mobile phones are much in use, group members can practise ringing up and telling someone exactly where they are.

- Keeping safe and how to say 'no'. This is a sensitive subject, as it must not be the intention to alarm young people unduly. However, they do need reminding about not doing anything they feel is wrong or worrying. This topic can provide opportunities for role play and links to personal, social and emotional education.

- Family events such as bereavement, divorce, births and weddings can be topics for discussion.

- Bullying and teasing. It should be borne in mind that young people with social communication difficulties can be the perpetrators of bullying as well as the victims. This may be connected with a skewed perception of friendship. Fixed ideas about this can result in uncompromising responses that are little different from bullying and teasing. Any physical assault should be taken very seriously indeed, and dealt with in the context in which it occurs. Serious incidents need specialised intervention, which is beyond the scope of a social skills group.

- How do I look? This may be appropriate for older children and young people who may be seeking work experience or employment. Video-recording can provide a useful means of evaluating body language, dress, communication skills and so on. Role play can be used to simulate an interview situation.

- Public information. Road signs, safety signs, washing and dry cleaning symbols can be looked at and interpreted. Cleaning materials, medicine information and warnings can also be explored.

- Substance abuse, including smoking and drugs. This is an important and wide-ranging topic that could certainly cover several sessions.

Before embarking on these add-on topics, it is advisable to seek out resources as well as specialised information that could be put to use. It is implicit that there will be close liaison with teaching staff involved with curriculum development in these areas.

FINAL WORDS

We are very aware of the pressures already in existence on both teachers and speech & language therapists. Taking on the running of social skills groups may seem like an initiative too far. However, we would advocate doing just this for a number of very sound reasons:

- There are too many children around with social communication difficulties, with or without a diagnosis, struggling or having problems in mainstream schools.

- Social skills groups are a practical and cost-effective way of meeting their needs.

- There is increasing interest in the teaching of social skills to this group of children.

- If nothing specific is offered, parents tend to make unrealistic demands for approaches that are both expensive and of dubious value in the long term.

- A social skills approach appeals to parents for the right reasons. They are active participants, and are generally extremely supportive. (See Parent Evaluation Forms, Appendix I.)

- This approach has proved very popular with group members, and is stimulating and enjoyable for those running the groups.

- It is effective because it is based on research findings relating to social understanding and communication.

Part V

Appendixes

Appendix I Forms

Appendix II Resources

APPENDIX I

Forms

We have included some sample forms that may be used as presented or adapted to suit individual circumstances.

Form 1 – Application/Referral for Social Skills Group/Baseline Information. The aim is to provide essential information on individual children to ensure a suitable mix within each group.

Form 2 – Letter to Parents. This informs parents that their child has a place in a group, and includes an invitation to a parents' workshop session. It includes an information sheet, and a form for parents to fill in to give information about their child.

Form 3 – Progress Profile for Group Leaders. This is for the use of those running the group, and can be filled in quickly after each session.

Form 4a – Progress Profile for Parents. This simple checklist is aimed at the parents of children between the ages of 5 and 11, to enable them to monitor progress in the areas of social communication that are the focus of the group sessions.

Form 4b – Homework Tasks for 7–11 year-olds. Parents' information sheet.

We suggest that parents of 'early years' children use their worksheets to record progress.

Forms 5a and 5b – Evaluation Forms for Parents. These forms will enable parents of children in the younger age groups to record their views on the overall success of the group. *Form 5a* will be completed when the group ends, and *Form 5b* – a much simpler form – six months later. The onus will be on parents to return the second form. *Form 5a* has been designed so that the information can be used for audit purposes.

Form 6 – Self-Evaluation Form. This is for older children and adolescents to reinforce their perceptions of what has been achieved in the group, and what they got out of it.

Forms 7a, 7b and 8 – Forms/Letters For Teachers. These are aimed at teachers who are not directly involved with the running of groups, but have participating children in their class or school. We are very aware of the fact that teachers are already bombarded with more paperwork than they can handle. However, it is necessary to keep them informed of what the groups are working on, and whether the children they know are achieving any of the goals. *Form 7b* may be used by teachers as a framework for establishing a baseline in order to evaluate the child's progress after the final group session.

Form 1 – APPLICATION/REFERRAL FOR SOCIAL SKILLS GROUP/BASELINE INFORMATION

Social Skills Group

Referred by
eg, SLT, HV, Cl Psych, Ed Psych, Teacher
(please denote)

Date

Child's name

Date of birth

Address

Tel no

School/Nursery

NB: Child must be in school/nursery and be able to separate from parents.

List relevant episodes of intervention – *eg, SLT, OT*.

SEN status

Other relevant information (*eg, medical history*)

Attention (*please tick*)   Level 1 ☐   Level 2 ☐   Level 3 ☐   Level 4 ☐
fleeting ⟵⎯⎯⎯⎯⎯⎯⟶ integrated

LANGUAGE/COMMUNICATION

Describe the child's difficulties with communication and list any assessment results.
NB: Applications should only be made for children whose difficulties centre on the use of language, not its acquisition.

BEHAVIOUR

Give a brief description of the child's behaviour.

Form 2 – LETTER TO PARENTS

Social Skills Group

Date _____

Dear _____

We are pleased to offer your child _____ a place in a Social Skills Group at _____. The group will meet for _____ sessions on _____ from _____ to _____ starting on _____ and ending on _____.

As places in the group are limited and we have a waiting list, it is essential that parents only accept a place if they feel able to commit themselves to bringing their child to all sessions. Occasionally, a child may not settle in a group, or may find it difficult to cope if they are not yet ready for this kind of input. In such circumstances, we may suggest that the child is withdrawn.

There will be a Parent Workshop Session to discuss the aims of the group at _____ on _____ from _____ to _____. It is essential that you attend this session.

Please sign and return the slip below by _____.

We do hope your child will be able to attend.

Yours sincerely _____

---- ✂ --

To _____
_____

Re: Social Skills Group from _____ to _____

I would/would not like my child _____ to attend this group, and I will/will not attend the workshop session.

I understand that video recordings may be made of some of the group sessions.

Signed _____

Name of parent _____

Contact telephone no _____

Form 2 – LETTER TO PARENTS continued

How do you see your child?

SOCIAL SKILLS GROUP

Date _____

Name of child _____

Date of birth _____

School/nursery _____

1 What do you feel is your child's biggest problem in relation to communication?

2 What other difficulties give you cause for concern?

3 Is it difficult to manage your child's behaviour? Please describe.

4 What would you like your child to gain from attending a group?

5 What do you hope to gain for yourself?

Form 2 – LETTER TO PARENTS continued

Parent Workshop Social Skills Group

INFORMATION

The aim of the group is to develop your child's social understanding and use of language.

Many of the younger children attending the group will have a good naming vocabulary, and may be able to use quite advanced language when making comments, or talking about things that are of interest to them. However, their language may have a learnt or derived quality, and perhaps includes snippets of videos and echoed phrases which they find pleasing in some way. It is the conversational and interactive aspects of communication that present problems for them. Older children may have difficulty in understanding humour, ambiguity and metaphorical language. They may have problems making friends and knowing how to behave appropriately in unfamiliar situations. They will be encouraged to take part in role play as a means of developing strategies to cope with these difficulties.

In order to develop social communication skills, group activities will focus on listening, appropriate looking and eye contact, attention fixing and turn-taking. 'Snack time', when a drink and biscuit will be offered, will be an important component of the sessions. It encourages children to make choices, and develops their awareness of the needs and interests of others. Snack time for older children will be organised by the young people themselves.

If your child has any food allergies please let us know.

If you are the parent of a young child, you will be invited to participate in a group session, if appropriate, to observe the activities so that you can reinforce them at home. You will also be asked to cooperate in simple 'homework' tasks/coursework, and to talk about the group with your child in between sessions. After the last group session, you will have an opportunity to discuss your child's progress and a brief written report will follow.

We hope there will be liaison with your child's school or nursery, as social skills and social communication need to be encouraged and developed at all times, and in all situations.

The workshop is an opportunity for you to share your concerns about your child, which will help us to address his or her particular needs.

Form 3 – PROGRESS PROFILE FOR GROUP LEADERS

Social Skills Group

Rating scale   1 = Poor attention/lack of cooperation
2 = Variable attention/cooperation
3 = Sustained attention/cooperation

Child's name _____

Willingness to participate

Date		Date		Date		Date	
Scale		Scale		Scale		Scale	
Date		Date		Date		Date	
Scale		Scale		Scale		Scale	

Attention control

Date		Date		Date		Date	
Scale		Scale		Scale		Scale	
Date		Date		Date		Date	
Scale		Scale		Scale		Scale	

Turn-taking

Date		Date		Date		Date	
Scale		Scale		Scale		Scale	
Date		Date		Date		Date	
Scale		Scale		Scale		Scale	

Response to/interest in other children

Date		Date		Date		Date	
Scale		Scale		Scale		Scale	
Date		Date		Date		Date	
Scale		Scale		Scale		Scale	

Overall behaviour

Date		Date		Date		Date	
Scale		Scale		Scale		Scale	
Date		Date		Date		Date	
Scale		Scale		Scale		Scale	

Speechmark   This page may be photocopied for instructional use only. *Social Skills Programmes* © M Aarons & T Gittens 2003

Form 3 – PROGRESS PROFILE continued

Comments

Summary of progress

Recommendations

Form 4a – PROGRESS PROFILE FOR PARENTS

Social Skills Group

Please use this form to make a brief comment about your child's response to each session, and to the homework tasks. Please note any changes or developments in your child's social communication skills.

Session 1. Date

_____

Session 2. Date

_____

Session 3. Date

_____

Session 4. Date

_____

Session 5. Date

_____

Session 6. Date

_____

Session 7. Date

_____

Session 8. Date

_____

Session 9. Date

_____

Session 10. Date

Form 4b – PARENTS' INFORMATION SHEET

Homework Tasks for 7–11 year-olds

Session 1 Help your child fill in his or her calendar with family birthdays, weekly activities and any events.

Session 2 Ask your child to think of situations when good manners are especially important.

Session 3 Help your child list six words and phrases that indicate good manners, eg, 'please'.

Session 4 Help your child find pictures in papers and magazines showing people enjoying doing things together.

Session 5 Find a photograph of another child considered to be a friend or get your child to draw a picture of him or her.

Session 6 Help your child to fill in a worksheet about favourite things.

Session 7 Help your child find pictures in papers and magazines showing a range of different feelings.

Session 8 Help your child fill in a worksheet with a list of idioms so that he understands their meaning, and add a new idiom to the list.

Please send in a small financial contribution for a special snack time in two weeks' time – the final session.

Session 9 Help your child fill in a worksheet about what he or she has gained from coming to the group.

We will be having our special snack time in the next session.

Form 5a – EVALUATION FORM FOR PARENTS

Social Skills Group

Please mark the appropriate box with a cross, and write clearly in black ink in the comments boxes.

1a **Did your child ever talk about the group at home?** ☐ Yes ☐ No

1b **If yes, was your child**
                                                                                  Yes   No
    (a) Enthusiastic about the group?   ☐ ☐
    (b) Indifferent to the group?   ☐ ☐
    (c) Bored with the group?   ☐ ☐

2 **Did your child respond to being reminded about the aims of the group (for example, listening attentively)?** ☐ Yes ☐ No

3 **How much progress in using language socially has your child made since attending the group?** (Please mark the appropriate box on the scale from 0 = no progress to 10 = exceptional progress)
☐ 0 ☐ 1 ☐ 2 ☐ 3 ☐ 4 ☐ 5 ☐ 6 ☐ 7 ☐ 8 ☐ 9 ☐ 10

4 **Did you attend the initial parents' session?** ☐ Yes ☐ No

5 **If yes, did you find this session**
☐ Very helpful? ☐ Helpful? ☐ Neither helpful nor unhelpful? ☐ Unhelpful? ☐ Very unhelpful?

6 **Overall, how do you think your child has found the group?**
☐ Very helpful? ☐ Helpful? ☐ Neither helpful nor unhelpful? ☐ Unhelpful? ☐ Very unhelpful?

7 **If a further group was offered, would you like your child to attend?** ☐ Yes ☐ No

8a **Are there any things not covered in the group that you would like to see covered in the future?** ☐ Yes ☐ No

8b **If yes, please list them in the box below.**

9 **If you have any further comments or suggestions about the group, please enter them in the box below.**

THANK YOU FOR TAKING THE TIME TO COMPLETE THIS FORM

This page may be photocopied for instructional use only. *Social Skills Programmes* © M Aarons & T Gittens 2003

Form 5b – FOLLOW-UP EVALUATION FORM FOR PARENTS

Social Skills Group

Please complete and return this form about six months after your child's last group session.

Child's name

1 When did your child attend a group?

2 Do you feel that your child has maintained the progress that he or she made during the group?

3 Has anyone else mentioned that your child has made progress? (*eg, class teacher, grandparents*)

4 Do you feel that your child has stayed much the same?

5 Has your child regressed in any way?

6 Overall, do you feel that your child has benefited from attending a social skills group? If possible, please give an example.

7 Would you like your child to attend another group if one is offered in the future?

THANK YOU FOR TAKING THE TIME TO COMPLETE THIS FORM

Please return to:

This page may be photocopied for instructional use only. *Social Skills Programmes* © M Aarons & T Gittens 2003

Form 6 – SELF-EVALUATION FORM

Social Skills Group

(You can ask a parent or teacher to help you fill this in.)

Name

1 Did you enjoy coming to the group?

2 What did you find particularly difficult before coming to the group?

3 Now do you find this: ☐ Easier? ☐ The same?

4 What particular things did you like about the group?

5 What particular things did you not like about the group?

6 Did you make any new friends in the group?

7 Did you develop any new interests from attending the group?

8 If given the chance, would you like to attend another group?

WHEN YOU HAVE COMPLETED THIS FORM, PLEASE GIVE IT TO YOUR GROUP LEADER. THANK YOU.

  This page may be photocopied for instructional use only. *Social Skills Programmes* © M Aarons & T Gittens 2003

Form 7a – LETTER TO SENCO

Social Skills Group

Date _____

To SENCO _____

School _____

Name of child _____

This child has a place in a Social Skills Group at _____ for _____ weekly sessions lasting about one-and-a-half-hours. These will start on _____.

The group will focus on aspects of social communication such as:

- Self-awareness and awareness of others
- Listening
- Turn-taking
- Observation and looking
- Group interaction skills

We hope that you will be able to support _____ in using these skills in school.

You will receive further information either directly or via the child's parents. A report will be written after the last session, and you will be asked to fill in a form to enable us to ascertain whether progress has been made. From then on we will liaise with you to consider any future needs the child may have in relation to social skills.

Social Skills Group
How teachers can help

1 While the child is attending the group, it might be possible to encourage him or her to talk to you a little about the weekly sessions. We can provide you with information about their format, as can the child's parents. You can simply remind the child of his or her attendance at the group by mentioning the name of the person running the group.

2 Encourage the child to report back to the group about something he or she has succeeded at in school. Say: 'You can talk about that when you give your news.' The child's parents could be involved with this in order to make it work.

3 Children with social communication difficulties often find it easier to elaborate on someone else's statement than answer an open-ended question: for example, 'I expect you have been to your group this week ... did you play any good games?', rather than 'What did you do at your group?'

4 If possible, reinforce the concepts of 'good looking' and 'good listening' at appropriate times in the school day. The child may be helped if he or she is reminded at the start of an activity such as assembly, circle time, news time, story time, and so on.

5 Using the child's name before making a request or suggestion helps to focus his or her attention on what is required. Some children will be unaware that when the teacher addresses the whole class, they are included.

6 The use of phrases such as 'good looking' and 'good listening' is specifically applied in order to try to promote positive reinforcements for acceptable behaviour.

7 Children with social communication problems often have fluctuating attention, and so find it easier to respond to simple, rule-based approaches that do not involve convoluted explanations.

8 The child may not see the point of pleasing the teacher, and so needs clear and simple explanations of what is expected in terms of his or her behaviour.

9 Often the child will find the unstructured situations in school, such as playtime, difficult to cope with, especially if he or she finds social interaction difficult. Suggestions as to what games could be played; which areas of the playground have special designations; who to go to for help, and so on, might help to diffuse problems. Similarly, the child might need to have the format of 'wet play' made clear.

Form 7a continued

10 Children with social communication difficulties often have a poorly developed idea of 'what happens next' and the sequence of the daily timetable. They may be helped if they are prepared for changes in advance with very simple explanations that emphasise 'before' and 'after', and are linked to their specific roles. For example, 'After you have finished you will be able to ...'

11 Changes in the school day, visits, outings, end-of-term parties, and so on may also need to be presented to the child in advance with very simple explanations. Changes in routine are often treated with suspicion by children with social communication difficulties.

12 Some children with a diagnosis of an autistic spectrum disorder have well-developed specific skills – for example, computing, reading or drawing, that could perhaps be utilised more in lessons so that the child begins to develop an awareness of his or her role within the class. However, it is obvious that these skills must be kept in perspective and not allowed to dominate either that child's behaviour or the rest of the class.

13 Emphasise the importance of the child looking at you when he or she speaks, and also when listening.

14 Keep instructions simple and unambiguous. Bear in mind that the child may have little idea of what to focus on or what is relevant. Therefore he or she may have great difficulty extracting information and using it meaningfully.

15 Try to keep your language fairly concrete. Try to avoid metaphor; sarcasm that may not be understood, and too many colloquialisms.

16 Emphasise the importance of turn-taking, and check that the child really understands what the concept of 'turns' means.

17 Reinforce any work on feelings, so that the child begins to consider not just the basic ones, such as 'happy', 'cross' and 'sad', but also 'fed up', 'tired', 'annoyed', and so on, and how other people feel.

18 Some children with a diagnosis of an autistic spectrum disorder may appear aggressive towards other children. Sometimes this is because they want to be friends, but do not know how to go about it and use inappropriate strategies.

  This page may be photocopied for instructional use only. *Social Skills Programmes* © M Aarons & T Gittens 2003

Form 7b – OBSERVATION IN CLASS

Social Skills Group

(Please score 0-4 on a scale from 0 = no difficulty to 4 = considerable difficulty.)

Name _____ Date of birth _____ Chronological age _____

Date _____

Length of time observed _____

Type of activity/lesson observed:

- ☐ Sitting
- ☐ Looking
- ☐ Listening
- ☐ Turn-taking
- ☐ Interest in/focus on topic
- ☐ Behaviour
- ☐ Participation/contribution
- ☐ Awareness of others
- ☐ Spontaneous social communication
- ☐ Voice quality/speech difficulty
- ☐ Response to teacher's instructions
- ☐ Number of interruptions

Comments:

Form 8 – EVALUATION FORM (PROFESSIONALS)

Social Skills Group

Name of child _____

The above-named child has recently attended a _____ week social skills group.

In order to monitor his or her progress, it will be helpful if you could complete this questionnaire. The parents know that we are contacting you.

1 Were you aware that this child was attending a social skills group?

2 Have you noticed any changes in this child over the past few weeks in relation to:
  a Communication?

  b Play?

  c Relationships with other children?

  d Motivation and task completion?

  e Ability to attend and focus?

3 Any comments:

Thank you for your help. Please return this questionnaire in the SAE which is enclosed.

Resources

APPENDIX II

One of the great advantages of running social skills groups is the fact that recommended resources are generally already available to most speech & language therapists, as well as teachers of children with special needs. Apart from a few specific recommendations, we continue to suggest that it is the *kind* of resource rather than specific titles that is important, because books go out of print and are superseded by more up-to-date and interesting material. Indeed, children's publishing and educational titles are flourishing and we are spoilt for choice. We continue to encourage readers to browse regularly through catalogues, high street shops, and in particular bookshops specialising in remaindered publications. Special needs exhibitions continue to provide opportunities to view the latest titles, posters and equipment.

We still particularly like the following books, and although we cannot guarantee that they are all still in print, most should be available.

BOOKS

Ahlberg A & Ahlberg J, 1978, *Each Peach Pear Plum*, London: Viking.
Aliki, 1994, *Feelings*, London: Macmillan Children's Books.
Aliki, 1994, *Manners*, London: Mammoth.
Aliki, 1995, *Communication*, London: Mammoth.
Bradman T, 1989, *Look Out, He's Behind You*, London: Mammoth.
Damon E, 1995, *All Kinds of People*, London: Tango Books.
Goffe T (illus), 1991, *Bully for You*, Swindon: Child's Play.
Gray C, 2001, *The New Social Story Book*, Arlington: Future Horizons, 2001.
Hawkins C & Hawkins J, 1992, *Max and the School Dinners*, London: Viking.
Ironside V, 1996, *The Huge Bag of Worries*, Hove: Macdonald Young Books.
Kelly A, 1996, *Talkabout*, Bicester: Speechmark Publishing.
Kelly A, 2003, *Talkabout Activities*, Bicester: Speechmark Publishing.
Liu G & Green J, 1999, *How do you feel?*, London: Evans Brothers Ltd.
Moses B & Gordon M, 1993, *Your Emotions* series. Titles include: *I Feel Sad, I Feel Angry, I Feel Jealous, I Feel Frightened*, Hove: Wayland.
Moses B & Gordon M, 1997, *Your Emotions* series. Titles include: *I'm Bored, I'm Lonely, I'm Worried, It's Not Fair, It Wasn't Me, I Don't Care, Excuse Me, I'll Do It*, Hove: Wayland.
O'Neill C & Goffe T, 1993, *Relax*, Swindon: Child's Play.
Rosen M & Oxenbury H, 1993, *We're Going on a Bear Hunt*, London: Walker Books Ltd.
Schroeder A, 1996, *Socially Speaking*, Wisbech: Wisbech LDA.
Smith C, 2003, *Writing & Developing Social Stories*, Bicester: Speechmark Publishing.
Suhr M, & Gordon M, 1993, *The Senses* series. Titles include *Hearing, Sight, Taste, Smell, Touch*. Hove: Wayland.

POSTERS

Good Talking and Good Listening, Maggie Johnson, 2001, Leicester: Taskmaster Resources 2001.

VIDEOS

Writing Social Stories with Carol Gray, 2001, Arlington: Future Horizons.

EQUIPMENT

For turn-taking activities with young children, a selection of small toys is especially useful. These should be visually appealing, move and make a noise, so that they provide an incentive for the children to engage with them for a short period of time, before being required to hand them on.

Speechmark's *ColorCards®* are highly recommended because of their visual appeal and versatility. For older children *Social Situations, Problem Solving* and *Emotions* are especially useful.

SPECIAL NEEDS SUPPLIERS

United Kingdom

Learning Development Aids
Park Works
Norwich Road
Wisbech
Cambridgeshire PE13 2AE
Publish a mail-order catalogue for students with special needs

NFER-Nelson
Darville House
2 Oxford Road East
Windsor
Berks SL4 1DF

The Paget-Gorman Society
Materials are available from
Stass Publications
44 North Road
Ponteland
Northumberland NE20 9UR
Tel 01661 822316
Fax 01661 860440
E-mail susan@stass.demon.co.uk

Speechmark Publishing Ltd
Telford Road
Bicester
Oxon OX26 4LQ
Produce ColorCards®, including sequencing cards and many books for children and adolescents with special needs. Catalogue available.

Taskmaster Ltd
Morris Road
Leicester
LE2 6BR

Winslow/Rompa
Goyt Side Road
Chesterfield
Derbyshire S40 2BR
Mail order catalogue of special needs resources

Australia
Modern Teaching Aids
26-28 Chard Road
Brookvale
NSW 2100
Educational catalogue of resources suitable for students with special needs

Canada
Braut & Bouthillier
700 Avenue Beaumont
Montreal H3N 1V5
www.brautbouthillier.com
Educational catalogue featuring toys and many items for teachers of children with special needs

Psycan Corp
Unit 12
120 West Beaver Creek Road
Richmond Hill
Ontario L4B 1L2
Distributors of materials for speech & language therapy

United States of America
Future Horizons
721 West Abram Street
Arlington
Texas 76013
Catalogue of resources for autism and Asperger's Syndrome

S&S Worldwide
75 Mill Street
PO Box 513
Colchester
Connecticut 06415
Games and educational toys catalogues

The Speech Bin
1965 Twenty-fifth Avenue
Vero Beach
Florida 32960
Mail-order catalogue with workbooks and picture cards for speech & language pathologists

Super Duper Publications
PO Box 24997
Greenville
South Carolina 29616-2497
www.superduperinc.com
Range of workbooks and games for all children with special needs

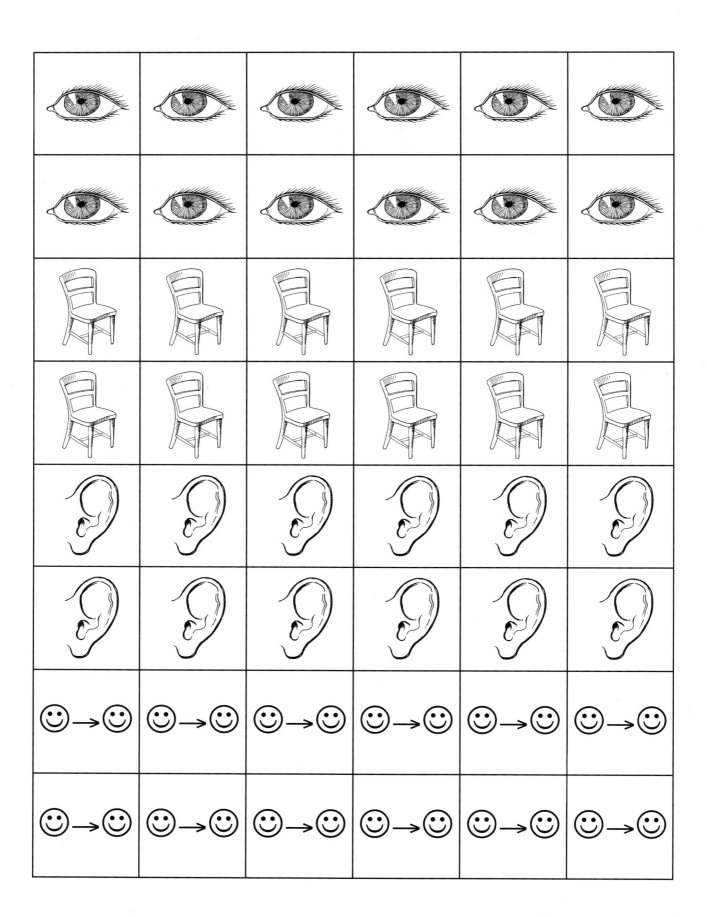

CERTIFICATE OF ACHIEVEMENT

_____ has attended a social skills group for _____ sessions. He/she is now able to

_____

_____

He/she is trying hard to remember to _____

_____

Well done!

Signed _____